Martin Nordin

MUSHROOMS

**Over 70 recipes that celebrate
our favourite fungi**

Hardie Grant
BOOKS

CONTENTS

GLORIOUS MUSHROOMS!

'Mushrooms! Glorious mushrooms! Oh, how I love mushrooms!' That might sound like a silly line from a children's song of the 70s, but that's really how I feel.

This book is about cooking mushrooms. Because it's true – I love mushrooms. In all their forms. And I have done so for as long as I can remember. My mother used to make creamy mushroom soup during the week, and at the weekends and for celebrations we would have mushroom-stuffed mushrooms, creamy mushroom mince on croustades, mock snails and some kind of sauce or stew smelling of white wine. In all of these, I remember the mushrooms more than any other ingredient. And that, I suppose, is the genesis for this book. Much of the food that I cook features mushrooms as a component – perhaps not always as the main ingredient, sometimes starring as the understudy in a broth or as another flavour agent.

But this isn't a book about how to pick mushrooms – there are plenty of great books all about that topic already. I own several of them and frequently dream of going out into the woods and finding my own mushroom treasures at an undisclosed location that can be returned to year after year when in season. And it goes without saying that I would love to feel absolutely confident about which mushrooms I can eat, while avoiding picking those that should remain untouched in nature. So if you feel the same way, I recommend that you buy a book like that.

Most of the mushrooms in this book are cultivated. Cultivation is beginning to take place on a larger scale than before. This means that you will find a wider variety of mushrooms in the supermarket and that even mushrooms that were previously imported from distant Asia (such as shiitake) are now grown in many different countries. In this respect, everything from major mushroom farms to smaller urban growers and the grow-it-yourself trend have really taken off. The oyster mushroom is one of the easier ones to cultivate, while other varieties – like shiitake, nameko and so on – require more specific conditions, including precise temperatures and special light. And we've still not found a way to cultivate mushrooms like chanterelles. But isn't it exciting to have mushrooms that are still predominantly led by the seasons and conditions in nature?

In recent years, I have been particularly inspired by the cuisines of Asia – Japan, Korea, Vietnam, Thailand and Taiwan – largely due to their techniques and thinking around balancing flavours and textures. Of course, I am also fascinated by Nordic cookery as a whole, with a particular penchant for the dairy heartlands of southern Sweden and the county of my childhood, Skåne, which is where all my memories of my mother's and my grandmothers' food are set. As I grew up, I developed an interest in French and Italian food thanks to restaurant visits, and later when my passion grew further, thanks to cookery shows and books, they were joined by the rest of the world. However, Asia is perhaps just ahead of the pack, meaning that I often end up with a mix of everything and a little too much soy sauce.

I've also chosen to make all the recipes in this book completely plant-based, so if you are a vegan then you can get cracking too. If you want to substitute a nut butter or milk for dairy-based milk or cream, or if you prefer to use regular butter instead of oil, then that's fine. After all, the inspirations for several of these dishes would have originally used dairy. You're the head chef in your own kitchen – it's up to you! I just hope that I can inspire you to create some new flavour memories!

The mushrooms we eat

With the exception of chanterelles and porcini, virtually all the mushrooms that we buy in stores are cultivated. (Porcini mushrooms are actually the world's most widely used non-cultivated mushroom in commercial settings.) So how does this work? Well, in order for mushrooms to grow we need mycelium – a root-like network that supplies the fruiting body with nutrients – and a substrate in which the mushrooms can grow. The substrate can really be anything from compost and sawdust to straw, logs or even coffee grounds. Then it is vital to find the right temperature and light conditions to ensure that the mushrooms are happy. Then, hey presto, you have a mushroom farm. In the case of some mushrooms that are easier to cultivate, it's perfectly possible to buy what you need and try it at home for yourself.

Given that many of the mushrooms in this book are cultivated, there is no need to clean and trim all of them. However, do pay attention to those that are grown wild or cultivated in soil (such as champignons, chanterelles and porcini). With these varieties, be sure to brush off any earth and cut away any parts that appear to be damaged beore using them for cooking.

The healthy mushroom

Mushrooms are not only delicious, they are also fantastically healthy. It's therefore no surprise that mushrooms have become a regular fixture in plant-based cookery. They also have a powerful umami flavour that means they are a good meat alternative.

All mushrooms are incredibly low in fat but rich in essential minerals and nutrients. The champignon is rich in vitamin B, iodine, potassium and iron. What's more, it is the mushroom that is best for our immune systems. Champignons are actually one of the few non-animal foodstuffs to contain vitamin B12. Vitamin B12 is primarily found in animal-based foods such as meat and fish, as well as some dairy products. Foods that have been fermented – that have been proved and which contain lactic acid – also usually contain a little vitamin B12.

Chanterelles are not only beautiful and tasty, they also contain a lot of useful nutrients, such as proteins and plenty of dietary fibre, which help the digestion. In addition, there are healthy minerals like selenium, manganese, zinc, calcium and iron. And don't forget that chanterelles are rich in vitamin C and D. However, the vitamin C disappears if the mushrooms are cooked, although vitamin D is always preserved when cooking. Vitamin D is good for our skin and our immune systems, while also making a contribution to preventing osteoporosis.

I'm not going to go over all the types of mushrooms here, but if you want to know more about the most common mushrooms that are cultivated and sold, then search on the internet for mushroom growers near you and explore their websites.

Which mushroom should I choose?

The number of mushroom species that are available is constantly on the rise. I really do urge you to be bold and try making the dishes in this book using your favourite mushroom. Here is a compilation of the mushrooms that I buy frequently, with a few words on their characteristics and how I use them.

Champignons

Champignons are the most widely cultivated mushrooms in the world. They have a mild flavour and are beautifully aromatic. When the cap of the closed, immature champignon parts from the stem, making the gills visible, it has a very full-bodied flavour.

Chestnut mushrooms

Sometimes referred to as forest or brown champignons, these are more full-bodied in flavour than their regular champignon cousins, with a pronounced flavour and a distinctive texture.

Portobello mushrooms

Portobello mushrooms are chestnut mushrooms that have been allowed to grow and mature for a few more days. They are typified by a firmer consistency and so they are great for cooking in bigger chunks that bring a magnificent balance of texture to a dish.

Porcini mushrooms

I think porcini mushrooms are a delicious ingredient in sauces, soups, stews and much more. You can also dry them for long-term storage and, once they are dried, they are great mushrooms for flavouring things like broths and mayonnaise (just like their umami sibling the shiitake) or can be used as mushroom salt on popcorn (page 152).

Nameko mushrooms

When raw, the nameko mushroom has a peppery acidity that becomes pronounced on the tastebuds after 30–60 seconds in your mouth. When fried, it has a light acidity and nutty flavour that is reminiscent of cashew nuts.

King oyster mushrooms

The king oyster mushroom is an oyster mushroom featuring the same nutty taste. However, it also has a big, fat stem that is great to work with, while being characterised by a chewy, meaty texture that can be ideal if you are looking for a different consistency in your dish. It all boils down to how you chop and cook it.

Shiitake mushrooms

These mushrooms have the most umami of all, which is further enhanced if you dry them and use them as a flavouring agent in broths. The cap is tender while the stem is sinewy in texture. They are fantastic when marinated, pickled or fermented, or when simply fried upside down.

Oyster mushrooms

The grey oyster mushroom is found in most major supermarkets, although the pink and yellow ones are not as readily available. It grows in bunches and is characterised by its mild, slightly nutty flavour. The oyster mushroom is excellent for frying on a high heat or deep frying as it takes on a lovely, crispy consistency and all the nutty flavour blossoms.

Pioppino mushrooms

This mushroom has a slightly meaty, firm texture and smells almost floral. It is nutty, peppery and ever so slightly sweet in taste.

Chanterelle mushrooms

The chanterelle mushroom grows in both deciduous and coniferous forests and is widely found in mountain birch forests. This means the mushrooms absorb sugars while growing, giving them a flavour of their own – peppery and spicy.

Black morel mushrooms

Black morels have picked up something of a bad reputation of late, but this is probably the fault of the false morel, which can cause acute poisoning. Black morels are edible, but there have been a handful of known (albeit mild) poisoning cases. In several of these cases, large quantities of mushrooms were consumed and it is possible that they had also been insufficiently heated or not cooked for long enough. You should always cook black morels at a high temperature for at least 15 minutes, and you should never eat them in large quantities.

Winter chanterelle mushrooms

These grow late in the autumn, making their name something of a misnomer as they stop growing after the first heavy frost. They are just as tender and even milder than their chanterelle siblings, and do not require as much time to cook.

BOILED MUSHROOMS

A classic, delicious champignon soup is pretty hard to beat, but there are actually many more dishes and ways that you can use mushrooms when popping them in a saucepan or soup bowl. Thanks to their umami riches, mushrooms are the perfect flavour agent in a range of broths that you can then use as a base and supplement with other tasty ingredients.

But you can also top a yummy soup with finely sliced fresh mushrooms, giving a completely different mouthfeel to that offered when it has been cooked in the dish from the beginning.

01

CREAMY **MUSHROOM** SOUP WITH TAHINI, MISO AND CASHEWS

600 g (1 lb 5 oz) mushrooms
2 tablespoons rapeseed (canola)
   oil, plus extra for drizzling
45 g (1¾ oz) finely chopped
   spring onions (scallions)
1 tablespoon finely chopped
   garlic
1 tablespoon mirin
1 tablespoon cashew butter
   (page 167)
1 tablespoon tahini
1 teaspoon light miso
100 ml (3½ fl oz/scant ½ cup)
   roasted mushroom broth
   (page 160) or vegetable stock
   (page 160)
200 ml (7 fl oz/scant 1 cup)
   cashew milk or alternative nut
   milk, or regular cow's milk

FOR THE SPICE MIX
2 teaspoons gochugaru
   (mild Korean chilli)
1 tablespoon nutritional yeast
1 tablespoon toasted white
   sesame seeds
1 teaspoon sea salt flakes
1 tablespoon roasted buckwheat
   (page 172)

FOR SERVING
3 small baguettes
2 tablespoons rapeseed (canola)
   oil
Sichuan pepper oil

1. Trim, clean and finely slice the mushrooms. Pour the oil into a saucepan and put on a medium heat. Add the mushrooms, spring onions and garlic and fry until the spring onions are soft without taking on any colour. Add the mirin, then add the cashew butter, tahini and miso and stir to ensure everything is mixed properly. Add the broth and cashew milk, lower the heat slightly and leave to simmer on a low heat until everything has reduced down a little.

2. Add all the ingredients for the spice mix except the buckwheat to a food processor and pulse until it is well mixed. Pour the mix into a bowl, add the buckwheat and stir.

3. Cut the baguettes lengthways, drizzle a little oil over them and rapidly grill or fry cut-side down. Place a baguette slice in a bowl, ladle some of the mushroom soup over it and top with the spice mix and a few splashes of Sichuan pepper oil.

SOUR RED CABBAGE AND BEETROOT SOUP WITH **SHIITAKE MUSHROOMS** AND GRILLED BREAD

3 tablespoons peanut (groundnut)
   oil or rapeseed (canola) oil
300 g (10½ oz) shiitake mushrooms
salt

FOR THE SOUR RED CABBAGE
AND BEETROOT SOUP
600 g (1 lb 5 oz) red cabbage
   sauerkraut (page 157)
1 tablespoon peanut (groundnut)
   oil
2 silverskin onions, finely sliced
   (yellow or red onions are
   also fine)
1 tablespoon finely chopped garlic
1 tablespoon red wine vinegar
100 ml (3½ fl oz/scant ½ cup)
   juice from the sauerkraut
600 ml (20 fl oz/2½ cups)
   roasted mushroom broth
   (page 160) or vegetable stock
   (page 160)
200 ml (7 fl oz/scant 1 cup)
   beetroot juice
200 ml (7 fl oz/scant 1 cup)
   dry apple cider
salt

FOR SERVING
3 small baguettes
2 tablespoons rapeseed (canola)
   oil

1. Begin with the soup. Let the sauerkraut drain in a sieve, making sure you save the juice for later. Pour the oil into a saucepan and put on a medium heat. Add the sauerkraut, onions and garlic and fry until everything is soft without having taken any colour. Add the vinegar and stir to ensure it is mixed thoroughly. Add the sauerkraut juice, broth, beetroot juice and apple cider. Lower the heat slightly and simmer on a low heat until it has all reduced down slightly.

2. Heat the oil in a frying pan (skillet) on a high heat until it begins to smoke. Add the mushrooms and fry on a high heat for about 10 minutes until they colour.

3. Cut the baguettes lengthways, drizzle a little oil over them and rapidly grill or fry cut-side down. Pour the soup into bowls, top with mushrooms and serve with the bread.

MISO SOUP WITH **KING OYSTER MUSHROOMS**, QUINOA AND SEAWEED

SERVES 6

300 g (10½ oz) king oyster
   mushrooms, finely sliced
500 g (1 lb 2 oz) cooked quinoa

FOR THE MISO BROTH
2 carrots
2 spring onions (scallions)
3 garlic cloves
400 ml (13 fl oz/generous
   1½ cups) cold water
800 ml (28 fl oz/3½ cups)
   shojin dashi (page 161)
100 ml (3½ fl oz/scant ½ cup)
   light miso
10 g (½ oz) dried toothed wrack
   or nori
sea salt

FOR SERVING
spring onions (scallions), finely
   chopped
radish sprouts

1. Begin with the miso broth. Finely chop the carrots, spring onions and garlic (or it's also fine to use a food processor). Set the light parts of the spring onions to one side for now and put the carrot, garlic and dark green parts of the spring onions in a large saucepan. Add the cold water and bring to the boil. Lower to a medium heat, add the dashi and miso and leave to cook for 15 minutes. Strain the broth.

2. Rinse the saucepan and return the broth to the pan. Add the seaweed, cover with a lid and leave to stand for 15 minutes. If the miso broth has cooled down too much, then bring it back to the boil immediately before serving. Season with salt but remember that the seaweed may well have added more salt to the broth, so add to taste.

3. Divide the quinoa evenly among the serving bowls. Remove a little seaweed from the broth and place it on top. Fill each bowl with the miso broth and top with the king oyster mushrooms, the salad onions you kept aside and the radish sprouts.

MUSHROOM BROTH WITH RICE, ROASTED KALE AND FRESH **CHAMPIGNONS**

SERVES 6

FOR THE MUSHROOM
BROTH
600 g (1 lb 5 oz) mushrooms
1 medium yellow onion
1 small carrot
1 leek, the green part
2 litres (67 fl oz/8 cups)
   cold water
3 garlic cloves
2 bay leaves
2 teaspoons of black peppercorns
3 sprigs of parsley
2 sprigs of thyme
sea salt flakes

FOR THE ROASTED KALE
200 g (7 oz) kale
2 garlic cloves
2 tablespoons cooking oil
sea salt flakes and black pepper

FOR SERVING
450 g (1 lb) cooked, hot
   long-grain rice
300 g (10½ oz) mushrooms
watercress
Sichuan pepper oil

1. Begin with the broth. Finely chop the mushrooms, onion, carrot and the dark green part of the leek (it's also fine to use a food processor). Put the vegetables in a large saucepan, pour over the cold water and bring to the boil. Crush the garlic and add to the saucepan along with the bay leaves and black peppercorns. Lower the heat and leave to simmer for 45 minutes.

2. Remove the pan from the heat. Add the parsley and thyme and stir a few times. Cover with the lid and leave to stand for 20 minutes. Strain and season with a little salt.

3. Heat the oven to 120°C (250°F/gas ½). Cut off the stem of the kale if it is thick and woody. Place the leaves and garlic cloves in a baking tray (pan) and drizzle with the oil. Season with salt and pepper. Roast in the middle of the oven for 20–25 minutes. Take out the cabbage from the oven and place on a draining rack.

4. Add a few spoonfuls of rice to each bowl. Finely slice a few mushrooms and add on top. Fill each bowl with broth and top with the roasted kale, watercress and a few drops of Sichuan pepper oil.

Tip Hang on to the mushroom and vegetable mix from the broth – it works well as a filling in dumplings (page 33).

SWEDE WITH CHERVIL BROTH, SILVERSKIN ONIONS AND **KING OYSTER MUSHROOMS**

SERVES 6

1.2 litres (40 fl oz/4¾ cups)
    classic light mushroom broth
    (page 160) or vegetable stock
    (page 160)
50 g (2 oz) chervil
1 teaspoon apple cider vinegar
salt
2 large swedes (rutabagas),
    about 1 kg (2 lb 4 oz)
600 g (1 lb 5 oz) king oyster
    mushrooms
2 silverskin onions, finely sliced
1 tablespoon finely chopped
    garlic
3 tablespoons rapeseed (canola)
    oil, for frying

FOR SERVING
3 tablespoons of whisky-pickled
    mustard seeds (page 172)
1 sprig of chervil
1 lemon, cut into wedges

1. Bring the broth to the boil, add a sprig of chervil (saving some for garnish) and add the vinegar. Remove from the heat and leave to stand with the lid on for 20 minutes. Strain and season with salt.

2. Peel the swedes and cut into thin slices, preferably using a mandoline to ensure they are as thin as possible. Cut the mushrooms into small cubes.

3. Heat the oil in a frying pan (skillet) on a high heat until it begins to smoke. First, add the mushrooms and fry on a high heat for about 5 minutes until they begin to colour. Lower to a medium heat and add the onions and garlic. Stir for about 5 minutes until it becomes soft without the onion colouring. Add the mushroom broth, then add the slices of swede and leave to simmer gently for 15–20 minutes until the swede is soft.

4. Remove the swede using tongs and add a little to each bowl. Ladle out the mushroom and onion broth before topping with pickled mustard seeds and chervil. Serve with lemon wedges on the side.

CREAMY WHITE BEANS AND **OYSTER MUSHROOMS** SAUTÉED IN WHITE WINE

SERVES 6

2 tablespoons olive oil
600 g (1 lb 5 oz) oyster
  mushrooms, grated into strips
200 ml (7 fl oz/scant 1 cup)
  white wine
salt

FOR THE CREAMY WHITE
BEANS
2 tablespoons rapeseed (canola)
  oil
75 g (2½ oz) finely chopped
  shallots
1 tablespoon finely chopped
  garlic
1 tablespoon white wine vinegar
1 tablespoon cashew butter
  (page 167)
600 g (1 lb 5 oz) cooked
  cannellini beans
100 ml (3½ fl oz/scant ½ cup)
  classic light mushroom broth
  (page 160) or vegetable stock
  (page 160)
200 ml (7 fl oz/scant 1 cup)
  cashew milk
2 teaspoons rice flour
1 teaspoon nutritional yeast

FOR SERVING
parsley
sea salt flakes
olive oil

1. Begin with the beans. Pour the rapeseed oil into a saucepan and put on a medium heat. Add the shallots and garlic and fry until everything is soft without having taken on any colour. Add the vinegar and cashew butter and stir a few times. Add the beans and continue to stir until everything is thoroughly mixed. Add the remaining ingredients, lower the heat slightly and leave to simmer on a low heat until everything has reduced down and is creamy in consistency.

2. Heat the olive oil in a frying pan (skillet) over a medium heat. Add the mushrooms while constantly stirring the pan and turning the mushrooms for about 10 minutes until they colour. Add the wine and leave to simmer until the wine has been completely reduced. Season with salt to taste.

3. Serve on plates with a generous scoop of white beans at the bottom followed by the oyster mushrooms. Top with parsley and salt flakes, before finishing with a few drops of olive oil.

PITCH-BLACK DUMPLINGS FILLED WITH **SHIITAKE AND PORTOBELLO MUSHROOMS,** COURGETTE, CARROTS, SPRING ONIONS AND GINGER

SERVES 6

FOR THE PITCH-BLACK
DUMPLING DOUGH
8 g (¼ oz) activated charcoal powder
  (page 177)
200 ml (7 fl oz/scant 1 cup) lukewarm
  water
320 g (11 oz) plain (all-purpose) flour
¼ teaspoon salt

FOR THE STUFFING
1 litre (34 fl oz/4 cups) water
about 20 g (¾ oz) dried shiitake
  mushrooms
150 g (5 oz) courgette (zucchini)
75 g (2⅓ oz) carrots
50 g (2 oz) spring onions (scallions)
200 g (7 oz) portobello mushrooms
1 tablespoon grated ginger root
1½ tablespoons light Chinese soy
  sauce (sheng-chou)
about ½ teaspoon salt
¼ teaspoon white pepper
1½ teaspoons sesame oil

FOR THE SAUCE
4 tablespoons light Chinese soy sauce
  (sheng-chou)
2 teaspoons sesame oil
2 tablespoons black Sichuan vinegar
1 garlic clove, finely grated
1 tablespoon cane sugar or caster
  (superfine) sugar
1 teaspoon Sichuan pepper oil

FOR SERVING
radish sprouts
black garlic salt

1. Add the charcoal powder to half of the water and stir with a spoon before leaving to stand for a few minutes. Work the black water together with the flour and salt. Then add the remaining water a little at a time and knead the dough for about 3 minutes until smooth. Leave to rest under a tea towel (dish towel) at room temperature for 40–60 minutes.

2. Bring the water to the boil, remove from the heat and add the dried shiitake. Cover with the lid and leave to stand for around 15 minutes. Grate the courgette and carrots and finely slice the spring onions. Remove the shiitake from the water, squeeze them and dry off any excess water. Finely chop the shiitake and portobello mushrooms and place in a bowl together with the other ingredients for the filling. Stir to ensure that everything is well mixed.

3. Roll out the dough into a long sausage, about 3 cm (1¼ in) thick, then divide it into 60 pieces. Work with one hand on the rolling pin while turning the dough in quarter turns between each roll of the pin using your other hand until you have small, round dumpling circles, about 8 cm (3¼ in) in diameter. Cover them in a tea towel until it is time to fill them.

4. Make the sauce. Whisk together the soy sauce, sesame oil, vinegar, garlic and sugar. Pour into a serving bowl and drip a little Sichuan pepper oil over the top.

5. Place a heaped tablespoon of filling in the middle of the dough circle. Moisten the edge with a little water, fold over and pinch the edges together. Repeat the process with the remaining dough. Add plenty of water to a pan and bring to the boil. Cook the dumplings in batches, leaving them to boil for 3–4 minutes. When they begin to float to the surface, leave them to cook for around another 30 seconds, then lift out with a draining spoon.

6. Serve beside the dipping sauce, cut a few radish sprouts over the dish and top with black garlic salt.

DUMPLINGS WITH **OYSTER MUSHROOMS, CHAMPIGNONS**, CABBAGE, PEPPER AND CHIVE STUFFING

SERVES 6

FOR THE DUMPLING DOUGH
200 ml (7 fl oz/scant 1 cup)
   lukewarm water
330 g (11 oz/2⅔ cups) plain
   (all-purpose) flour
¼ teaspoon salt

FOR THE STUFFING
1 litre (34 fl oz/4 cups) water
60 g (2 oz) dried oyster
   mushrooms
200 g (7 oz) mushrooms
125 g (4 oz) pointed cabbage
¼ teaspoon white pepper
¼ teaspoon black pepper
2 bird's eye chillies
50 g (2 oz) spring onions
   (scallions), finely chopped
20 g (¾ oz) wild garlic leaves,
   finely sliced
1 tablespoon grated ginger root
1½ tablespoons light Chinese soy
   sauce (sheng-chou)
½ teaspoon vinegar
1½ teaspoons toasted sesame oil
about ½ teaspoon salt

FOR SERVING
crispy chilli oil, such as
   Lao Gan Ma
radish sprouts

1. To make the dough, work half the lukewarm water with the flour and salt to make a paste, then add a little water at a time and knead the dough for about 3 minutes until smooth. Leave to rest under a tea towel (dish towel) at room temperature for 40–60 minutes.

2. For the stuffing, bring the water to the boil, then remove from the heat and add the oyster mushrooms. Cover with the lid and leave to stand for 15 minutes. Grate the pointed cabbage. Remove the oyster mushrooms from the water, squeeze them and dry off any excess water. Finely chop all the mushrooms. Use a mortar to crush the pepper and chillies. Add all the ingredients for the filling to a bowl and mix well.

3. Roll out the dough into a long sausage, about 3 cm (1¼ in) thick. Then divide it into 60 pieces. Work with one hand on the rolling pin while turning the dough in quarter turns between each roll of the pin using your other hand until you have small, round circles, about 8 cm (3¼ in) in diameter. Cover them in a tea towel until it is time to fill them.

4. Take a heaped tablespoon of filling and place in the middle of a circle of dough. Moisten the edge with a little water, fold over and pinch the edges together. Heat the oil in a frying pan (skillet) over a medium heat. Add as many dumplings as will fit. Wait for around 30 seconds, then add around 75 ml of water. Cover with a lid, raise the heat a little and leave to steam for about 3 minutes. Then remove the lid and cook until the water boils off and the underside of the dumplings is crispy.

5. Serve on a plate beside the chilli oil. Top with some radish sprouts.

FRIED MUSHROOMS

Frying is a classic technique for drawing different flavours out of many ingredients, and mushrooms are no exception. As a general rule, you should always start with a really hot pan. I prefer to use cast iron or carbon steel because they allow you to reach higher temperatures and offer a beautiful frying surface, and I usually opt for hot-pressed oil which deals well with hot temperatures, such as rapeseed (canola) or peanut (groundnut) oil.

An expensive, cold-pressed virgin olive oil can all too easily assume a pungent, metallic taste when it reaches high temperatures, and is best kept for use in cold vinaigrettes. A short frying time delivers a soft consistency, while frying for longer gives you harder, crispier mushrooms.

02

FRIED, MARINATED **SHIITAKE MUSHROOMS** WITH GREEN PEAS AND SHALLOTS

SERVES 6

600 g (1 lb 5 oz) shiitake
   mushrooms
6 shallots
2 tablespoons rapeseed (canola)
   oil

FOR THE MISO AND MALT
VINEGAR MARINADE
1 tablespoons light miso
1 tablespoon malt vinegar
1 teaspoons toasted sesame oil
1 teaspoon date syrup
1 tablespoon rapeseed (canola)
   oil

FOR SERVING
800 g (1 lb 12 oz) green peas,
   fresh or frozen
mint
pea shoots
salt and black pepper

1. Begin with the marinade. Add all the ingredients to a bowl and whisk together with a fork.

2. Clean and prepare the mushrooms. Peel the shallots and cut them in half. Heat the oil in a frying pan (skillet) on a high heat until it begins to smoke. Add the shallots cut-side down and fry on a high heat for about 5 minutes until they begin to colour and are slightly browned.

3. Turn over the shallots and add the mushrooms. Fry for another 5–10 minutes until the mushrooms begin to colour and look slightly golden brown. Lower to a medium heat, add the marinade and stir a few times to ensure everything is covered. Take off the heat.

4. Bring a pan of salted water to the boil, add the peas and cook fresh for 2–3 minutes or frozen according to the package instructions, then drain.

5. Add a generous serving of peas, onions and mushrooms to each plate. Top with mint, pea shoots, salt and freshly ground black pepper.

Tip: I usually boil peas in generously salted water to make sure they retain their verdant shade of green.

MISO- AND SESAME-SAUTÉED **PIOPPINO MUSHROOMS** AND ASPARAGUS ON A PITCH-BLACK BAGUETTE

300 g (10½ oz) pioppino
   mushrooms
300 g (10½ oz) asparagus
2 tablespoons rapeseed (canola) oil

FOR THE MISO AND SESAME
OIL MIX
2 tablespoons light miso
1 tablespoon mirin
2 teaspoons toasted sesame oil
1 tablespoon cold-pressed peanut
   (groundnut) oil

FOR SERVING
3 small baguettes (for pitch-black
   Polish baguettes, page 168)
serrano chilli, finely sliced
dill
cold-pressed peanut (groundnut) oil

1. Put the ingredients for the miso and sesame oil mix into a bowl and whisk using a fork.

2. Clean the mushrooms and asparagus.

3. Heat the oil in a frying pan (skillet) on a high heat until it begins to smoke. Add the mushrooms and fry on a high heat for about 5 minutes until they begin to colour.

4. Add the asparagus and lower to a medium heat. Fry the mushrooms and asparagus for about 10 minutes until they take on a nice colour. Make sure you stir them occasionally and keep an eye on them to ensure they do not burn. Add the miso and sesame mix and stir a few times to ensure everything is covered. Set to one side for now.

5. Cut the asparagus into 3 mm (⅛ in) slices, keeping the tips intact. Cut the baguettes lengthways and fry or grill them quickly, cut-side down. Place a generous serving of asparagus and mushrooms on each slice of baguette and then top with chilli, dill and a few drops of peanut oil.

CHAMPIGNON SANDWICH WITH WHISKY MAYONNAISE, WILD GARLIC AND TRUFFLES

SERVES 6

300 g (10½ oz) mushrooms
2 tablespoons rapeseed (canola)
   oil
6 thick slices of bread, crusts
   cut off
salt and black pepper

FOR THE WHISKY
MAYONNAISE
100 ml (3½ fl oz/scant ½ cup)
   aquafaba
1 tablespoon Dijon mustard
2 teaspoons whisky, preferably
   a honey-sweet Speyside
2 teaspoons malt vinegar
1 teaspoon salt
1 pinch of white pepper
500 ml (17 fl oz/2 cups) rapeseed
   (canola) oil (not cold pressed)

FOR SERVING
wild garlic leaves
chives, finely chopped
salt and black pepper
fresh truffle

1. Begin with the mayonnaise. Put all the ingredients except the rapeseed oil in a beaker or a tall, narrow bowl. Mix, using a hand-held blender, until everything is blended. Put the hand-held blender to the bottom of the bowl and add the rapeseed oil in a thin stream while mixing (hold the hand-held blender still at the bottom of the bowl). When you notice the mayonnaise starting to settle, pull the hand-held blender upwards. Continue mixing to a good consistency.

2. Clean the mushrooms and slice thinly. Heat the oil in a frying pan (skillet) on a high heat until it begins to smoke. Add the mushrooms and fry on a high heat for 10–15 minutes until they colour. Season with salt and pepper and set aside for now.

3. Brush both sides of each slice of bread with some oil. Heat the oil in a frying pan on a high heat, add the slices of bread and fry until golden brown on both sides.

4. Place a dollop of mayonnaise on each slice of bread and distribute the mushroom pieces across the sandwich. Add 1–2 leaves of wild garlic and some chives to each. Season with salt and pepper before finishing by shaving a little truffle on top.

SHOYU RAMEN WITH FRIED **KING OYSTER MUSHROOMS**, NOODLES, BROAD BEANS AND SHISO

300 g (10½ oz) broad (fava)
    beans
3 king oyster mushrooms
2 tablespoons rapeseed (canola)
    oil
300 g (10½ oz) ramen noodles
    (page 164)

FOR THE SHOYU BROTH
1 litre (34 fl oz/4 cups) shojin
    dashi (page 161)
2 cm (¾ in) ginger root, sliced
3 garlic cloves, lightly crushed
1 teaspoon coriander seeds
4 tablespoons Japanese soy
    sauce
2 tablespoons dry sake
1 tablespoon mirin, preferably
    hon mirin
20 g (¾ oz) shiso (perilla) leaves
    or mint leaves
20 g (¾ oz) coriander (cilantro)
    leaves

FOR SERVING
spring onions (scallions), finely
    chopped
shiso (perilla) leaves or mint
    leaves
coriander (cilantro) leaves
3 teaspoons sesame oil
3 teaspoons chilli oil

1. Begin with the broth. Bring the dashi to the boil with the ginger, garlic, coriander seeds, soy sauce and sake. Boil for around 15 minutes. Take off the heat. Add the mirin, then add the shiso and coriander. Stir a few times, cover with the lid and leave to stand for around 20 minutes. Strain the liquid.

2. Remove the broad beans from their pods. Put the beans in a saucepan and cover with water. Bring to the boil on a medium heat, then leave to simmer for about 10 minutes. Strain under cold running water. Remove the outer membranes from the beans and discard these. Set the beans to one side for now.

3. Cut the king oyster mushrooms into slices about 2 cm (¾ in) thick. Cut incisions into the mushrooms on both sides at 2 mm intervals, both horizontally and vertically, to create a grid pattern. Heat the oil in a frying pan (skillet) on a high heat until it begins to smoke. Add the mushrooms and fry on a high heat on both sides for about 10 minutes until they colour.

4. Add plenty of water to the pan and bring to the boil. Add the noodles and cook for 40 seconds. Strain and serve immediately.

5. Serve the noodles in deep dishes and pour a little warm broth over them. Top with the mushrooms, beans, spring onions, shiso, coriander and a few drops of sesame oil and chilli oil.

Tip: Hon mirin is an alcoholic mirin that it can be tricky to find, but if you encounter any while on your travels it is well worth bringing home.

FRIED **MORELS** WITH CREAMY WALNUT SAUCE, DEEP-FRIED WILD GARLIC AND AVOCADO OIL

SERVES 6

600 g (1 lb 5 oz) black morel
    mushrooms
30 g (1 oz) wild garlic leaves
rapeseed (canola) oil, for frying
sea salt

FOR THE WALNUT SAUCE
60 g (2 oz/⅔ cup) walnuts
500 ml (17 fl oz/2 cups) walnut
    milk (page 167), or alternative
    nut milk, such as unsweetened
    almond milk
2 tablespoons cashew butter
    (page 167)
sea salt and black pepper

FOR SERVING
avocado oil
black pepper spice
    (page 172)

1. Begin with the walnut sauce. Bring a saucepan of water to the boil on a high heat. Place a bowl of ice-cold water beside it. Blanch the nuts for about 10 seconds, then remove from the pan with a slotted spoon and place them in the cold water. Then remove as much of the skins as possible – I usually scrape them with the tip of a knife, which gets rid of most of it.

2. Add the nut milk to a saucepan and bring to the boil on a medium heat, then add the cashew butter and whisk until it is thoroughly mixed. Make the sauce airy by running a hand-held blender in it until it begins to get frothy. Add the walnuts and leave the sauce to simmer gently on a low heat for another 5 minutes. Season with salt and pepper to taste.

3. Clean the morels, cut them in half and ensure you clean them on the inside too. Set to one side for now.

4. Add plenty of oil to a frying pan (skillet), so that it comes up to about 1 cm (½ in) below the brim. Heat the oil to 180°C (350°F) and fry the wild garlic until it begins to bubble and takes on a deep green colour (take care to avoid it burning). Remove the wild garlic leaves and put on a paper towel to allow excess oil to drain off.

5. Remove a little of the oil from the frying pan, add the morels and fry for 3–4 minutes on each side until they are crispy and golden brown. Season with salt towards the end.

6. Place a few pieces of morel on each plate, pour the sauce over them and top with wild garlic leaves, avocado oil and black pepper spice.

PORTOBELLO MUSHROOMS AND KALETTES WITH CHIVES AND SWEET POTATO FRIES

600 g (1 lb 5 oz) portobello
    mushrooms
2 tablespoons rapeseed (canola)
    oil
300 g (10½ oz) kalettes (a cross
    between Brussels sprouts and
    kale)
salt and black pepper

FOR THE SWEET POTATO
FRIES
800 g (1 lb 12 oz) sweet potatoes
1–2 litres (34–67 fl oz/3–4 cups)
    peanut (groundnut) oil
1½ tablespoons cornflour
    (cornstarch)

FOR SERVING
chives, finely chopped
sea salt flakes
porcini mayonnaise
    (page 167)

1. Begin with the sweet potato fries. Peel the sweet potatoes and cut into batons, about 5 mm (¾ in) thick. Place them into a bowl of cold water for 30 minutes. Drain off the water and leave the batons on a tea towel (dish towel) until they are fully dried.

2. Add the oil to a saucepan with high edges and heat to 160°C (320°F). Fry one-third of the sweet potato batons at a time, for around 4 minutes per batch. Stir them using a slotted spoon while they are frying. Remove them and place into a metal colander to allow excess oil to drain off. Line them up on a baking sheet once they have cooled slightly and sprinkle with the cornflour.

3. Place a few layers of paper towel in a bowl. Heat the oil again until it has a temperature of 200°C (400°F). Now reduce to a medium heat and try to keep the temperature level at 200°C (400°F) as far as possible as you fry the sweet potato batons in three batches for around 3–4 minutes per batch, or until they are golden. Stir them using a slotted spoon while they are frying. Place the sweet potato batons on the paper towel to allow any excess oil to be absorbed. Season with salt and turn over.

4. Clean the portobello mushrooms and then cut into 1 cm (½ in) slices. Heat the oil in a frying pan (skillet) on a high heat until it begins to smoke. Add the mushrooms and fry on a high heat on both sides for about 5 minutes until they begin to colour. Add the kalettes and lower to a medium heat. Toss the mushrooms and kalettes until they take on a nice colour, for about 10 minutes.

5. Place some portobello mushroom and kalettes onto each plate and top with chives and salt flakes. Serve with porcini mayonnaise and sweet potato fries.

COLD TOMATO NOODLE SOUP WITH FRIED **SHIITAKE MUSHROOMS** AND PICKLED GOOSEBERRIES

SERVES 6

300 g (10½ oz) shiitake mushrooms
2 tablespoons rapeseed (canola) oil
1 teaspoon sesame oil
300 g (10½ oz) ramen noodles
  (page 164)

FOR THE PICKLED
GOOSEBERRIES
100 ml (3½ fl oz/scant ½ cup) vinegar
  (12%)
225 g (8 oz) caster (superfine) sugar
  or cane sugar
300 ml (10 fl oz/1¼ cups) water
2 finely chopped coriander roots
2 bird's eye chillies
½ teaspoon black pepper
½ teaspoon coriander seeds
½ teaspoon pink pepper
300 g (10½ oz) gooseberries

FOR THE COLD TOMATO SOUP
800 ml (28 fl oz/3½ cups) fermented
  yellow tomato sauce (page 157)
400 ml (13 fl oz/generous 1½ cups)
  shojin dashi (page 161)
1 teaspoon grated ginger root
1 tablespoon Japanese soy sauce
1 tablespoon mirin, preferably hon mirin

FOR SERVING
chives, finely chopped
Sichuan pepper oil

1. Start by pickling the gooseberries, preferably a day in advance. Boil the vinegar, sugar and water and stir until the sugar has dissolved. Add the spices, reduce the heat and leave to simmer for a few minutes, then strain the syrup. Top and tail the gooseberries and place them in a glass jar. Add the warm syrup, put the lid on the jar and put the jar in the refrigerator. After a few hours (and no more than 24 hours), the gooseberries should be ready.

2. Mix all the ingredients for the tomato soup, preferably using a food processor to ensure everything is mixed thoroughly.

3. Clean and prepare the mushrooms. Heat the rapeseed oil in a frying pan (skillet) on a high heat until it begins to smoke. Add the mushrooms and fry on a high heat for about 10 minutes until they colour. Lower the heat, add the sesame oil and then stir a few times to ensure that the oil covers all the mushrooms.

4. Add plenty of water to the pan and bring to the boil. Add the noodles and leave them for 40 seconds. Strain and serve immediately.

5. To serve, place the noodles in a deep dish and pour a little of the tomato soup over them. Top with the mushrooms, sliced gooseberries, finely chopped chives and a few drops of Sichuan pepper oil.

Tip: Coriander (cilantro) roots are the roots of the fresh herb you often find in Asian grocery stores rather than the kind you buy in a pot.

PASTA WITH FRIED **OYSTER MUSHROOMS** AND CREAMY BLACK KALE

600 g (1 lb 5 oz) oyster
    mushrooms
3 tablespoons rapeseed (canola)
    oil
600 g (1 lb 5 oz) fusilli

FOR THE SAUCE
4 tablespoons Japanese soy
    sauce
2 teaspoons sesame oil
2 tablespoons vinegar (12%)
1 tablespoon cane sugar or caster
    (superfine) sugar
1 garlic clove, crushed
1 red chilli, or equivalent amount
    of small, mild red chilli fruits,
    finely chopped
2 spring onions (scallions), finely
    chopped

FOR THE CREAMY BLACK KALE
250 g (9 oz) black kale
2 tablespoons rapeseed (canola)
    oil
75 g (2½ oz) finely chopped
    shallots
1 tablespoon finely chopped
    garlic
1 tablespoon sherry vinegar
2 tablespoons roasted mushroom
    broth (page 160) or vegetable
    stock (page 160)
1 tablespoon cashew butter
    (page 167)
1 teaspoon sesame oil

1. Start by putting the sauce ingredients in a bowl and whisking with a fork.

2. Cut off the stem from the black kale if it is thick and woody, then finely shred the leaves. Heat the oil in a frying pan (skillet) over a high heat. Add the black kale and shallots while constantly stirring the pan. Fry for 7–8 minutes while continuing to stir the pan. Then add the garlic and fry until it is all soft and has taken on some colour. Add the vinegar and let it sizzle for about 5 minutes. Then add the broth, cashew butter and sesame oil before stirring to ensure that everything is thoroughly mixed. Lower the heat slightly and simmer until it has all reduced down and the liquid has gone.

3. Clean the mushrooms. Heat the oil in a frying pan over a high heat. Add the mushrooms while constantly stirring the frying pan. Toss the mushrooms for about 10 minutes until they take on a nice colour. Add the mushrooms to the black kale.

4. Cook the pasta following the package instructions.

5. Place a generous helping of pasta on each plate. Top with the creamy black kale and mushrooms. Serve with the sauce on the side.

CREAMY PASTA WITH FRIED **MUSHROOMS** AND BRUSSELS SPROUTS

SERVES 6

600 g (1 lb 5 oz) mushrooms
3 tablespoons rapeseed (canola)
    oil
300 g (10½ oz) Brussels sprouts,
    halved

FOR THE CREAMY PASTA
600 g (1 lb 5 oz) pasta, such as
    campanelle
2 tablespoons rapeseed (canola)
    oil
75 g (2½ oz) shallots, finely
    chopped
1 tablespoon finely chopped
    garlic
1 tablespoon white wine vinegar
100 ml (3½ fl oz/scant ½ cup)
    roasted mushroom broth
    (page 160) or vegetable stock
    (page 160)
1 tablespoon cashew butter
    (page 167)
1 teaspoon nutritional yeast

FOR SERVING
chives, finely chopped
watercress
sea salt flakes

1. Begin with the pasta. Cook following the package instructions. Pour the oil into a saucepan and put on a medium heat. Add the shallots and garlic and fry until soft without taking on any colour. Add the vinegar and let it sizzle for about 10 minutes. Add the broth, cashew butter and nutritional yeast and stir a few times. Add the pasta and continue to stir until everything is thoroughly mixed. Lower the heat slightly and simmer until it has all reduced down and the liquid has gone.

2. Clean and slice the mushrooms. Heat the oil in a frying pan (skillet) over a high heat. Add the mushrooms, stirring constantly. Fry the mushrooms for about 10 minutes until they take on a nice colour. Add the mushrooms to the saucepan with the pasta and stir.

3. Add a little more oil to the frying pan, add the Brussels sprouts and fry them cut-side down until they colour. Lower the heat slightly, turn them over and fry for a little longer. Continue to fry them for another 10 minutes, stirring occasionally, until their leaves are crispy and they are slightly soft in the middle. Place on a draining rack to allow any excess oil to drain.

4. Place a generous helping of pasta and mushrooms on each plate, accompanied by the Brussels sprouts. Top with chives, watercress and a light sprinkling of salt flakes.

SWEET AND SOUR **NAMEKO MUSHROOMS** WITH FRIED TOFU AND SPRING ONIONS

SERVES 6

600 g (1 lb 5 oz) natural firm tofu

3 spring onions (scallions)

2 tablespoons rapeseed (canola) oil

300 g (10½ oz) nameko mushrooms

FOR THE SWEET AND SOUR SOY SAUCE

300 ml (10 fl oz/1¼ cups) shojin dashi (page 161)

100 ml (3½ fl oz/scant ½ cup) Japanese soy sauce

4 tablespoons semi-sweet sake

2 tablespoons mirin

1 tablespoon rice flour

FOR SERVING

pea shoots

radish sprouts

1. Start by squeezing any liquid out of the tofu. Wrap the tofu in a tea towel (dish towel) or paper towel, then place it on a chopping board with something under one end of the board so it is sloping on the diagonal. Place something heavy on the tofu – I usually use a heavy pan – and leave it to stand for about an hour. Then cut it into 6 equal pieces.

2. Cut the spring onions in half. Heat the oil in a frying pan (skillet) on a high heat until it begins to smoke. Add the spring onions cut-side down and fry on a high heat for about 5 minutes until they colour and are slightly burned. Lower the heat slightly, turn the onions over and fry them for another 10 minutes. Shake the frying pan occasionally and turn the spring onions again towards the end. Remove the spring onions and set aside.

3. Fry the tofu in the same frying pan for about 10 minutes until it has a nice colour on both sides. Remove the tofu and set aside on a draining rack so that any excess oil can drain off.

4. Lower the heat to a medium heat, add the mushrooms and the ingredients for the sweet and sour soy sauce. Bring to the boil and stir gently to ensure that everything is thoroughly mixed but without breaking the mushrooms.

5. Place a piece of tofu and spring onion on each plate, pour the nameko sauce over them and top with pea shoots, radish sprouts or any other herb that you like.

OVEN-ROASTED MUSHROOMS

Just like frying, roasting mushrooms is a way to deepen the flavours through the use of the Maillard reaction – the reaction between amino acids and sugars that gives browned food its distinctive flavour. However, in this case it is the dry, warm air that also concentrates the flavours in the mushrooms. And you can easily increase the intensity with the ingredients you add around your mushrooms, whether they are herbs, garlic or anything else that takes your fancy.

03

Roasted Mushrooms and Onions with Beer Broth (page 66).

ROASTED **MUSHROOMS** AND ONIONS WITH BEER BROTH

SERVES 6

600 g (1 lb 5 oz) mushrooms
3 teaspoons rapeseed (canola)
  oil
6 medium yellow onions
200 ml (7 fl oz/scant 1 cup) beer
  and lovage broth
Japanese soy sauce
rosemary
thyme

FOR THE BEER AND LOVAGE
BROTH
2 medium yellow onions
1 teaspoon black peppercorns
1 teaspoon coriander seeds
1 teaspoon Sichuan pepper
1.5 litres (50 fl oz/6 cups)
  vegetable stock (page 160)
500 ml (17 fl oz/2 cups) beer
  (lager or ale)
1 tablespoon malt vinegar
  (or white wine vinegar)
1 sprig of lovage
2–3 sprigs of parsley
1 sprig of thyme
sea salt

FOR SERVING
Sichuan pepper oil
thyme

1. Begin with the broth. Cut the onions in half and burn the cut edges in a really hot, dry frying pan (skillet). Add the onions, black pepper, coriander seeds and Sichuan pepper to the vegetable broth and beer in a large saucepan and bring to the boil. (Feel free to toast your spices first for a deeper flavour.) Leave to simmer for around 1 hour. Take off the heat. Add the vinegar and then add the lovage, parsley and thyme. Stir a few times, cover with the lid and leave to stand for 20 minutes. Strain and season with a little salt.

2. Heat the oven to 225°C (480°F/gas 9). Remove the mushroom stems (save them for making broth later). Heat the oil in a frying pan on a high heat until it begins to smoke. Add the mushrooms cap-side down and fry on a high heat for about 10 minutes until they colour. Cut the onions lengthways into either 2 or 4 pieces, depending on size. Place the mushrooms cap-side down together with the onions on a baking sheet. Fill all the mushrooms with 1–2 teaspoons of broth and few drops of soy sauce. Drizzle the oil over the onions, add a few sprigs of herbs and put the baking sheet in the oven. Roast for 10 minutes.

3. Fill deep bowls with about 300 ml (10 fl oz/ 1¼ cups) of broth. Add the mushrooms and onions and top with Sichuan pepper oil and a little fresh thyme.

Tip: While it's not for me to tell you how to eat your soup, I usually encourage people to eat the mushrooms and onions before then drinking the broth from the bowl. There's something that appeals to me about the texture of each bite, washed down with the broth afterwards. But it's up to you.

ROASTED **MUSHROOMS** WITH CANNELLINI BEANS IN BROTH

SERVES 6

600 g (1 lb 5 oz) mushrooms
3 teaspoons rapeseed (canola) oil
200 ml (7 fl oz/scant 1 cup) roasted
  mushroom broth (page 160)

FOR THE CANNELLINI BEANS
IN BROTH
3 medium onions
oil, for frying
sea salt flakes
4 medium coriander (cilantro) roots
  (see tip on page 55)
300 ml (10 fl oz/1¼ cups) roasted
  mushroom broth (page 160)
300 ml (10 fl oz/1¼ cups) kimchi
  juice (page 156)
300 g (10½ oz) cooked cannellini
  beans

FOR THE ROASTED KALETTES
200 g (7 oz) kalettes or Brussels
  sprouts
2 garlic cloves
2 tablespoons rapeseed (canola)
  oil
sea salt flakes and black pepper

FOR SERVING
serrano chilli, finely chopped
3 tablespoons whisky-pickled
  mustard seeds (page 172)

1. Begin with the broth and beans. Finely slice the onions and place in a cold saucepan. Drizzle with oil, then put the pan on a medium heat before adding some salt and then covering with a lid. The onions will soon start to release liquid and the flavours will be concentrated through the onions cooking in their own juices. Leave to cook for 10–15 minutes, stirring occasionally to ensure the onions do not burn.

2. Finely chop the coriander roots and add them to the onion slices, continuing to stir for a few minutes. Add the broth and kimchi juice, add the beans and then leave to simmer without the lid for another 15 minutes. Set to one side for now.

3. Heat the oven to 120°C (250°F/gas 1). Place the kalettes and garlic cloves on a baking sheet and drizzle with the oil. Season with salt and pepper. Roast them in the middle of the oven for 15–20 minutes. Remove from the oven and place on a draining rack.

4. Heat the oven to 225°C (480°F/gas 9). Remove the stems of the mushrooms. Heat the oil in an ovenproof frying pan (skillet) on a high heat until it begins to smoke. Add the mushrooms cap-side down and fry on a high heat for about 10 minutes until they colour. Fill them with 1–2 teaspoons of the mushroom broth and add a few drops of oil. Place the frying pan in the oven for 10 minutes.

5. Spoon generous helpings of broth and beans into deep plates, add a few spoonfuls of mushrooms and finally top with the kalettes, chilli and pickled mustard seeds.

MUSHROOMS

ROASTED **SHIITAKE MUSHROOMS**
IN SHOJIN DASHI

SERVES 6

600 g (1 lb 5 oz) shiitake
  mushrooms
3 garlic cloves, crushed with
  the skin on
3 tablespoons rapeseed
  (canola) oil
salt
1 teaspoon black pepper spice
  (page 172)

FOR THE BROTH
2 silverskin onions, skin on
1 litre (34 fl oz/4 cups) shojin
  dashi (page 161)
2 cm (¾ in) ginger root, sliced
1 cinnamon stick
1 star anise
2 tablespoons rice vinegar
1 pot of fresh coriander (cilantro)
salt

FOR SERVING
80 g (3 oz) bean sprouts
6 tablespoons spring onions
  (scallions), finely chopped
3 small, finely sliced green chillies
150 g (5 oz) green beans
  (haricots verts), thinly sliced
coriander (cilantro) leaves
Sichuan pepper oil
1 lime, cut into wedges

1. Begin with the broth. Cut the silverskin onions in half, leaving the skin on. Heat a dry frying pan (skillet) on a high heat and fry the onions cut-side down so that they burn. Add the onions, dashi, ginger, cinnamon stick and star anise to a saucepan. Bring to the boil, then leave to cook for about 15 minutes. Take off the heat. Add the vinegar and then the coriander. Stir a few times, cover with the lid and leave to stand for around 20 minutes. Strain and season with a little salt.

2. Heat the oven to 220°C (480°F/gas 9). Place the mushrooms and garlic in an ovenproof dish and drizzle with the oil. Season with salt and the black pepper spice. Turn the mushrooms with your hands to ensure that the oil and spice cover everything. Place the dish in the oven for about 20 minutes.

3. Distribute the bean sprouts across deep dishes, pour a little warm broth over them and top with spring onions, chilli, beans, coriander, mushrooms and a few drops of Sichuan pepper oil. Serve with the lime on the side.

MISO-FRIED, OVEN-ROASTED **PORTOBELLO MUSHROOMS** WITH PESTO AND FRIES

SERVES 6

900 g (2 lb) portobello
  mushrooms
2 tablespoons rapeseed
  (canola) oil
sprig of rosemary
4 garlic cloves, lightly crushed
  with the skin on
salt and black pepper

FOR THE PESTO
30 g (1 oz/scant ¼ cup) pine nuts
30 g (1 oz/scant ¼ cup) blanched
  almonds
60 g (2 oz) basil leaves
3 sprigs of rosemary
2 garlic cloves
1 tablespoon nutritional yeast
100 ml (3½ fl oz/scant ½ cup)
  olive oil
sea salt flakes

FOR THE MISO AND SOY
MARINADE
2 tablespoons dark miso
2 teaspoons tamari
1 tablespoon sherry vinegar
1 tablespoon rapeseed
  (canola) oil

FOR SERVING
French fries
nasturtium sprouts
sea salt flakes

1. Begin with the pesto. Heat a dry frying pan (skillet), preferably cast iron. Toast the nuts on a medium heat for around 2 minutes until they begin to colour. Shake the pan occasionally to make sure that the nuts don't burn too much. Then mix all the pesto ingredients using a hand-held blender or food processor. Season with salt.

2. Heat the oven to 225°C (480°F/gas 9). Add the ingredients for the miso and soy marinade to a bowl and whisk using a fork. Remove the stems from the portobello mushrooms and then cut them into 2 cm (¾ in) thick slices. Heat the oil in a frying pan on a high heat until it begins to smoke, then fry the mushrooms on a high heat on both sides for about 10 minutes so that they take colour. Turn off the heat, add the marinade and turn the pieces around to ensure everything is covered.

3. Place the mushrooms in an ovenproof dish, add a few sprigs of rosemary and the garlic cloves. Season with some salt and pepper. Roast in the middle of the oven for 10 minutes.

4. Serve the mushrooms straight from the oven together with freshly fried fries. Top with the pesto, sprouts and salt flakes.

ROASTED **MUSHROOMS** WITH PARSNIP AND MALT VINEGAR MAYONNAISE

12 small parsnips, trimmed
600 g (1 lb 5 oz) mushrooms
oil, for frying
200 ml (7 fl oz/scant 1 cup)
   vegetable stock (page 160)
1 sprig of rosemary
1 sprig of thyme
1 garlic clove

FOR THE MALT VINEGAR
MAYONNAISE
100 ml (3½ fl oz/scant ½ cup)
   aquafaba
1 tablespoon Dijon mustard
1 tablespoon malt vinegar
1 teaspoon salt
1 pinch of white pepper
500 ml (17 fl oz/2 cups) rapeseed
   (canola) oil (not cold pressed)

FOR SERVING
mild chillies, sliced, such as
   Espelette peppers
nasturtium sprouts
sea salt flakes

1. Begin with the mayonnaise. Put all the ingredients except the rapeseed oil in a beaker or a tall, narrow bowl. Mix, using a hand-held blender, until everything is blended. Put the hand-held blender to the bottom of the bowl and add the rapeseed oil in a thin stream while mixing (hold the hand-held blender still at the bottom of the bowl). When you notice the mayonnaise starting to settle, pull the hand-held blender upwards. Continue mixing to a good consistency.

2. Heat the oven to 225°C (480°F/gas 9). Spread out the parsnips in an ovenproof dish and roast in the middle of the oven for 20–25 minutes.

3. Remove the stems of the mushrooms. Heat a little oil in a cast-iron pan on a high heat until it begins to smoke. Add the mushrooms cap-side down and fry on a high heat for about 10 minutes until they colour. Fill the mushrooms with 1–2 teaspoons of stock, add a few herb sprigs and a whole crushed garlic clove. Put the pan in the oven and roast the mushrooms for 10 minutes.

4. Put a generous dollop of mayonnaise on a plate, spoon a few mushrooms and 1 or 2 parsnips on top. Finish with the Espelette pepper, sprouts and salt flakes.

DANISH PASTRIES WITH WHITE WINE–MARINATED **SHIITAKE MUSHROOMS**, DILL AND FURIKAKE

SERVES 6

2 tablespoons olive oil
300 g (10½ oz) shiitake
    mushrooms
200 ml (7 fl oz/scant 1 cup)
    white wine
salt
6 unbaked Danish pastries
    (page 168)
6 tablespoons plant-based crème
    fraîche

FOR SERVING
dill
furikake (page 142)
sea salt flakes

1. Heat the oil in a frying pan (skillet) over a medium heat. Add the mushrooms and fry for about 5 minutes, stirring, until they take on a little colour. Add the wine and leave to simmer until the wine has been completely reduced. Salt to taste.

2. Heat the oven to 200°C (400°F/gas 6). Get out the unbaked Danish pastries and brush a layer of crème fraîche on top. Top with the mushrooms and bake in the middle of the oven for 20–30 minutes until the pastries are crispy and golden brown.

3. Top with dill and furikake. Sprinkle some salt flakes over the top.

DANISH PASTRIES WITH SWEET POTATO SPREAD, **WINTER CHANTERELLES** AND FERMENTED YELLOW TOMATO SAUCE

SERVES 6

6 unbaked Danish pastries
   (page 168)
300 g (10½ oz) winter
   chanterelles

FOR THE SWEET POTATO
SPREAD
3 tablespoons rapeseed (canola)
   oil
500 g (1 lb 2 oz) sweet potatoes
3 garlic cloves
coarse sea salt
2 teaspoons white wine vinegar
salt and black pepper

FOR SERVING
oregano or marjoram
sea salt flakes
herb oil, preferably lovage oil
100 ml (3½ fl oz/scant ½ cup)
   fermented yellow tomato sauce
   (page 157)

1. Heat the oven to 200°C (400°F/gas 8). Begin with the sweet potato spread. Heat the oil in a frying pan (skillet) until it begins to smoke. Fry the sweet potatoes until the skins are crispy, verging on blackened. Place the sweet potatoes in an ovenproof dish together with the garlic, sprinkle some coarse sea salt on top and bake in the oven for around 45 minutes, or until the potatoes are completely soft. Remove and leave to stand until cool enough to handle. Cut the potatoes lengthways and carefully remove the flesh using a spoon, remove the skin from the garlic and mash everything roughly with a fork – it's great to have some chunky bits left. Add the vinegar, stir a few times and then season with salt and pepper.

2. Get out the unbaked Danish pastries and brush a layer of sweet potato spread on top. Top with the mushrooms and drizzle a little oil over them. Bake in the middle of the oven for 20–30 minutes until the pastries are crispy and golden brown.

3. Top with fresh oregano and sprinkle some salt flakes over them. Drip a little lovage oil over the fermented tomato sauce and serve alongside.

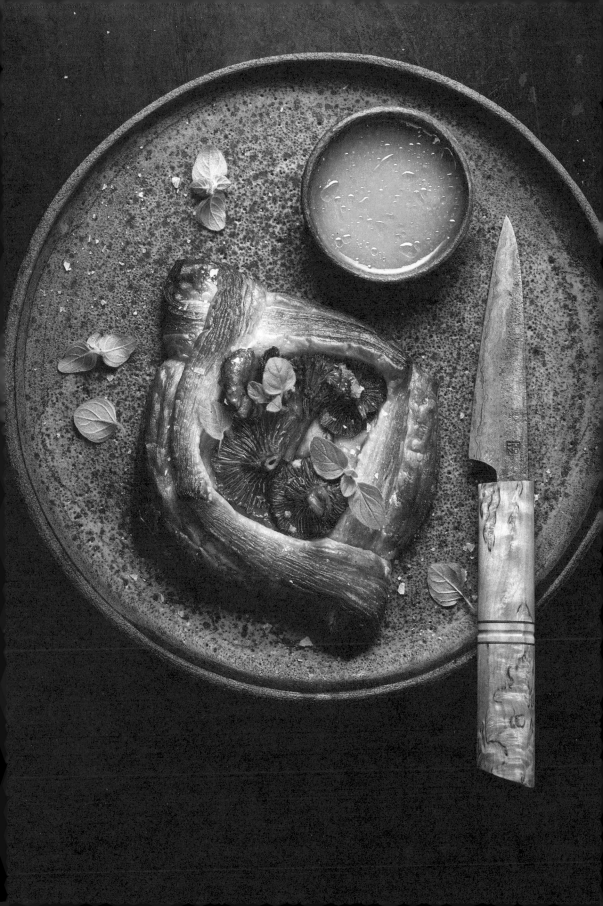

WHITE PIZZA WITH PUMPKIN, **CHANTERELLES** AND SHALLOTS

SERVES 6

2 medium shallots
1 small winter squash (such as
    uchiki kuri) or butternut squash
1 garlic clove
2 tablespoons olive oil
6 balls of Leve's pizza dough
    (page 169)
flour, for dusting
6 tablespoons plant-based crème
    fraîche
3 tablespoons pumpkin seed
    butter (page 167)
100 g (3½ oz) winter chanterelles

FOR SERVING
garlic oil
lovage
fermented yellow tomato sauce
    (page 157)

1. Heat the wood oven or regular oven with a pizza stone on the grill to the highest temperature possible. Leave for a while to ensure that the stone is really hot.

2. Peel the shallots and squash and cut into thin slices, preferably using a mandoline. Place the slices into a bowl, grate the garlic over them, add the oil and massage it in using your hands.

3. Dust a large chopping board generously with flour. Take a ball of the pizza dough and shape it into a round pizza. Let it rest for a few minutes. Dust the pizza paddle with flour, then place the pizza base on the paddle while pulling gently at the edges to make the circle bigger.

4. Take 1 tablespoon of crème fraîche and draw it out from the middle towards the edge in a thin layer. Drip a little pumpkin seed butter over it and spread it.

5. Add the slices of squash, shallot and winter chanterelles and put the pizza in the oven.

6. Once the edges of the pizza have bubbled up and taken on a good colour – it should preferably be a little burnt in places – it is ready. Remove from the oven and brush the edges with garlic oil and then top with lovage and a generous helping of tomato sauce.

WHITE PIZZA WITH KIMCHI AND **SHIITAKE MUSHROOMS** TOPPED WITH SWEET AND SOUR SESAME SAUCE

SERVES 6

flour, for dusting
6 balls of Leve's pizza dough
    (page 169)
6 tablespoons plant-based crème
    fraîche
3 tablespoons cashew butter
    (page 167)
300 g (10½ oz) kimchi
    (page 156)
600 g (1 lb 5 oz) shiitake
    mushrooms

FOR THE SWEET AND SOUR
SESAME SAUCE
3 tablespoons Japanese soy
    sauce
3 teaspoons sesame oil
1½ tablespoons vinegar (12%)
1 tablespoon agave syrup
2 teaspoons toasted sesame
    seeds

1. Heat the wood oven or regular oven with a pizza stone on the grill to the highest temperature possible. Leave for a while to ensure that the stone is really hot.

2. Whisk all the ingredients for the sauce together in a bowl.

3. Dust a large chopping board generously with flour. Take a ball of the pizza dough and shape it into a round pizza. Let it rest for a few minutes. Dust the pizza paddle with flour, place the pizza base on the paddle while pulling gently at the edges to make the circle bigger.

4. Take 1 tablespoon of crème fraîche and draw it out from the middle towards the edge in a thin layer. Drip a little cashew butter over it and spread it.

5. Add the kimchi and shiitake mushrooms before putting the pizza in the oven.

6. Once the edges of the pizza have bubbled up and taken on a good colour – it should preferably be a little burnt in places – it is ready. Remove from the oven and brush the edges with olive oil. Finish by drizzling a little of the sauce over it when serving.

FOCACCIA WITH KIMCHI AND
SHIITAKE MUSHROOMS

SERVES 6

FOR THE FOCACCIA DOUGH
1.3 kg (3 lb 5½ oz/8 cups) strong
   bread flour
1 litre (34 fl oz/4 cups) cold water
400 g (14 oz) active sourdough
40 g (2 tablespoons) clear honey
150 ml (5 fl oz/scant ⅔ cup)
   olive oil, plus a little extra for
   brushing
20 g (¾ oz) sea salt

FOR THE TOPPING
400 g (14 oz) kimchi
   (page 156), chopped
600 g (1 lb 5 oz) shiitake
   mushrooms
3 tablespoons Japanese soy
   sauce
3 teaspoons sesame oil
100 ml (3½ fl oz/scant ½ cup)
   olive oil

1. Mix the flour, water, sourdough and honey in a food processor fitted with a dough hook. Run at a medium speed for 10 minutes. Add the olive oil and salt and work the dough for another 5 minutes.

2. Get out a large plastic box, brush the sides and bottom with olive oil, add the dough and cover with the lid. Leave the dough to stand at room temperature with its lid on for 3–4 hours. Fold the dough once every 30 minutes while proving: moisten your hand and pick up the dough's outer edge, pull it carefully and fold it towards the middle. Continue until you have gone all the way around. Put the box containing the dough into the refrigerator until the next day.

3. Line an ovenproof dish with baking parchment, brush the paper generously with olive oil – too much is better than too little. Knock back the dough and spread it out by dipping your fingers in oil and then pressing the dough evenly into the dish. Wrap in cling film (plastic wrap) and leave in the refrigerator for a few hours – until the next day if possible.

4. Remove the dough from the refrigerator around 1 hour before it needs to go into the oven so that it can return to room temperature. Prepare the topping while you wait.

5. Heat the oven to 220°C (480°F/gas 9). Mix the ingredients for the topping in a bowl. Then gently apply pressure with your fingers across the dough to form holes which will bubble up. Take a handful of the mushroom and kimchi mix and drop into small heaps that are evenly distributed across the dough.

6. Place a bowl of water at the bottom of the oven. Place the dish in the middle of the oven and reduce the heat to 200°C (400°F/gas 8). Bake the focaccia for 20–25 minutes.

7. Remove the focaccia from the dish and place on a rack. Leave to cool for 30 minutes before serving.

FOCACCIA WITH HERB OIL
AND **OYSTER MUSHROOMS**

SERVES 6

focaccia dough (page 85)

FOR THE HERB OIL AND
OYSTER MUSHROOM TOPPING
800 g (1 lb 12 oz) oyster mushrooms
100 ml (3½ fl oz/scant ½ cup) olive
    oil
1 tablespoon white wine vinegar
30 g (1 oz) parsley, finely chopped
3 garlic cloves, finely chopped
1 mild red chilli, finely chopped
½ teaspoon dried oregano
1 teaspoon sea salt flakes

FOR THE CRACKED PESTO
MAYONNAISE
30 g (1 oz) pine nuts
30 g 1 oz) blanched almonds
60 g (2 oz) basil leaves
2 garlic cloves
1 tablespoon nutritional yeast
100 ml (3½ fl oz/scant ½ cup) olive
    oil
½ teaspoon sea salt flakes
200 ml (7 fl oz/scant 1 cup)
    mayonnaise

FOR SERVING
rocket (arugula)
parsley
thyme
radish sprouts

1. Prepare the focaccia dough by following the recipe on page 85, steps 1–4. Heat the oven to 220°C (480°F/gas 9).

2. Continue with the topping. If you don't feel up to it or don't have time to chop by hand, then it is fine to add everything to the food processor, but make sure you don't add the mushrooms. Mix the ingredients for the topping in a bowl. Then gently apply pressure with your fingers across the dough to form holes which will bubble up. Take a handful of the topping and drop in small heaps that are evenly distributed across the dough, applying gentle pressure to ensure that the mushrooms sink into the dough.

3. Place a bowl of water at the bottom of the oven. Place the dish in the middle of the oven and reduce the heat to 200°C (400°F/gas 8). Bake the focaccia for 20–25 minutes.

4. Remove the focaccia from the dish and place on a rack. Leave to cool for 30 minutes before serving.

5. Make the pesto mayonnaise while the focaccia cools. Heat a dry frying pan (skillet), preferably cast iron. Toast the nuts on a medium heat for around 2 minutes until they begin to colour. Shake the pan occasionally to make sure that the nuts don't burn too much. Then mix all the pesto ingredients except the mayonnaise using a hand-held blender or food processor. Add the pesto and mayonnaise to a bowl and stir carefully two to three times with a spoon.

6. Serve the focaccia with rocket, herbs, radish sprouts and the pesto mayonnaise on the side.

BARBECUE-GRILLED MUSHROOMS

Cooking on the barbecue grill is never as precise as frying or roasting. But it is much more fun and it delivers more flavour (depending, of course, on how you work with fire and smoke, and which fuel you use: gas, charcoal or wood). Usually when I grill mushrooms, I try to add a hint of smoke. I do this by adding some smoker chips to the barbecue grill towards the end and closing the lid. I generally always use chips from fruit trees – apple is a favourite – as I think this is often the best match to vegetables and mushrooms. It offers a slightly milder, rounder smoky taste.

04

Photo caption: Barbecue-Grilled, Marinated Mushrooms with Coleslaw and Pesto (page 92)

MUSHROOMS

BARBECUE-GRILLED, MARINATED
MUSHROOMS WITH COLESLAW AND PESTO

FOR THE COLESLAW
2 carrots (about 150 g (5 oz))
300 g (10½ oz) pointed cabbage
zest of 1 lemon
1 tablespoon lemon juice
2 pinches of salt
2 teaspoons Dijon mustard
100 ml (3½ fl oz) mayonnaise

FOR THE MARINATED
MUSHROOMS
600 g (1 lb 5 oz) mushrooms
4 tablespoons whisky
4 tablespoons rapeseed
   (canola) oil
2 tablespoons dark miso
2 tablespoons tamari
juice of ½ lime
1 tablespoon cane sugar
1 garlic clove
1 teaspoon sesame oil

FOR THE PESTO
30 g (1 oz/¼ cup) pine nuts
30 g (1 oz/¼ cup) blanched
   almonds
60 g (2 oz) basil leaves
2 garlic cloves
1 tablespoon nutritional yeast
100 ml (3½ fl oz) olive oil
sea salt flakes

FOR SERVING
bean sprouts
watercress

1. Begin with the coleslaw. Peel the carrots and clean the cabbage. Slice the carrots and cabbage finely, preferably with a mandoline. Add to a bowl and mix in the lemon zest, lemon juice and salt. Knead thoroughly with your hands. Leave to stand for about 20 minutes. Strain any liquid that has formed and finish by mixing in the mustard and mayonnaise.

2. Clean the mushrooms and break them down into bite-sized pieces. Thread the chunks onto skewers.

3. Mix all the remaining marinating ingredients using a hand-held blender or food processor. Brush over the mushrooms.

4. Continue with the pesto. Heat a dry frying pan (skillet), preferably cast iron. Toast the nuts on a medium heat for around 2 minutes until they begin to colour. Shake the pan occasionally to make sure that the nuts don't burn too much. Then mix all the pesto ingredients using a hand-held blender or food processor. Season with salt.

5. Light the charcoal in the grill and let it take on a fine, soft glow. Grill the mushroom skewers, occasionally turning them over and brushing them with a little more marinade. Once the mushrooms take on a nice, caramelised golden brown colour on the outside, they are done.

6. Place a helping of coleslaw on each plate. Remove the mushrooms from the skewers and place on top. Finish by topping with bean sprouts, watercress and the pesto.

KING OYSTER MUSHROOMS AND KIMCHI SKEWERS ON A BARBECUE-GRILLED SANDWICH

SERVES 6

150 g (5 oz) kimchi
6 large king oyster mushrooms

FOR THE MARINADE
juice from the kimchi
2 tablespoons chilli oil
4 tablespoons Japanese soy
   sauce
2 teaspoons sesame oil
1 tablespoon vinegar (12%)
1 tablespoon agave syrup

FOR THE SOY MAYONNAISE
100 ml (3½ fl oz/scant ½ cup)
   aquafaba
2 tablespoons Japanese soy
   sauce
1 tablespoon Dijon mustard
1 teaspoon vinegar (12%)
1 teaspoon sesame oil
500 ml (17 fl oz/2 cups) rapeseed
   (canola) oil (not cold pressed)

FOR SERVING
6 slices of white bread
spring onions (scallions), finely
   chopped
pickled radishes
chilli salt

1. Prepare the skewers, preferably a few hours prior to serving. Begin by straining/squeezing the juice from the kimchi. Mix the kimchi juice together with the other ingredients for the marinade in a bowl. Cut the king oyster mushrooms into 5 mm (¾ in) thick slices. Assemble the skewers by alternating between mushroom slices and pieces of kimchi. Then brush them with marinade.

2. Put all the ingredients for the mayonnaise except the rapeseed oil in a beaker or a tall, narrow bowl. Mix, using a hand-held blender, until everything is blended. Put the hand-held blender to the bottom of the bowl and add the rapeseed oil in a thin stream while mixing (hold the hand-held blender still at the bottom of the bowl). When you notice the mayonnaise starting to settle, pull the hand-held blender upwards. Continue mixing to a good consistency.

3. Light the charcoal in the barbecue grill and let it take on a steady, fine glow. Grill the mushroom skewers until they have a nice colour. Then apply indirect heat to them in the grill and roast them for about another 15 minutes.

4. Quickly grill the slices of bread on both sides. Spread a tablespoon of mayonnaise on each slice of bread, lay the mushroom skewer down on the sandwich and remove the skewer from the mushrooms. Top with spring onions, radishes and a pinch of chilli salt.

BARBECUE-GRILLED MUSHROOMS

BARBECUE-GRILLED **SHIITAKE MUSHROOMS** WITH KIMCHI AND JERUSALEM ARTICHOKE AND GARLIC SPREAD

SERVES 6

300 g (10½ oz) shiitake
   mushrooms
2–3 tablespoons rapeseed
   (canola) oil
salt and black pepper

FOR THE JERUSALEM
ARTICHOKE AND GARLIC
SPREAD
500 g (1 lb 2 oz) Jerusalem
   artichokes
3 garlic cloves
3 tablespoons rapeseed
   (canola) oil
2 teaspoons apple cider vinegar
coarse sea salt

FOR SERVING
3 small baguettes
150 g (5 oz) white kimchi,
   (page 156; classic red
   is also fine)
spring onions (scallions), finely
   chopped
watercress

1. Begin with the Jerusalem artichoke and garlic spread. Heat the oven to 200°C (400°F/gas 8). Add a layer of coarse salt to the bottom of an ovenproof dish and place the Jerusalem artichokes and garlic on the salt bed, ensuring there is a little distance between each piece. Sprinkle with coarse salt to ensure everything is covered. Bake in the middle of the oven for about 40 minutes until soft. Once the artichokes look slightly shrunken and grey on the outside, they are usually perfectly cooked on the inside. Peel the Jerusalem artichokes and garlic once they have cooled slightly. Place them in a food processor with the oil and vinegar. Season with salt and mix until it forms a smooth spread.

2. Clean the shiitake and cut them in half. Place them in a bowl with 2 tablespoons of the oil and a little salt and pepper, then mix to ensure they are properly covered. Place the mushrooms in a coarse-meshed strainer and put this on the barbecue grill or hold it over the glow. Occasionally shake the strainer and drip a little oil on at intervals. They are ready when they are a beautiful golden brown.

3. Cut the baguettes and rapidly grill them cut-side down. Spread a generous layer of Jerusalem artichoke and garlic spread onto each baguette, top with kimchi, shiitake mushrooms, spring onions and watercress.

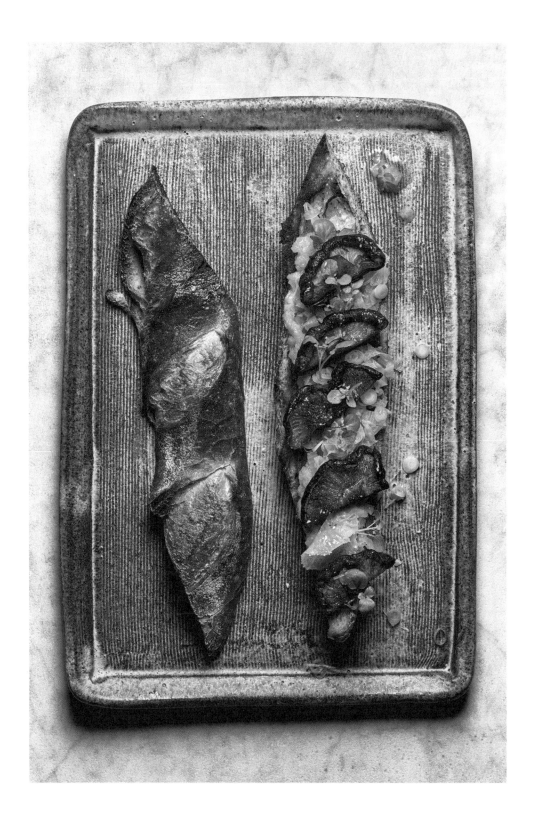

BARBECUE-GRILLED MUSHROOMS

BARBECUE-GRILLED, WHISKY-MARINATED
CHESTNUT MUSHROOMS ON A BAGUETTE

SERVES 6

300 g (10½ oz) chestnut mushrooms
skewers (soaked for 30 minutes if
   wooden)

FOR THE WHISKY AND MISO
MARINADE
4 tablespoons whisky, a mild Scotch
   or Japanese malt
4 tablespoons rapeseed (canola) oil
2 tablespoons dark miso
2 tablespoons tamari
juice from ½ lime
1 tablespoon cane sugar or caster
   (superfine) sugar
1 garlic clove
1 teaspoon sesame oil

FOR THE GARLIC MAYONNAISE
100 ml (3½ fl oz/scant ½ cup)
   aquafaba
3 garlic cloves
1 tablespoon Dijon mustard
2 teaspoons white wine vinegar
1 teaspoon salt
1 pinch of white pepper
500 ml (17 fl oz/2 cups) rapeseed
   (canola) oil (not cold pressed)

FOR SERVING
3 small baguettes
spring onions (scallions)
spring onion haulm powder

1. Prepare the skewers, preferably a few hours prior to serving. Mix all the marinade ingredients using a hand-held blender or food processor. Cut the mushrooms into 3 mm (⅛ in) thick slices, thread them onto skewers and brush them with the marinade. Place in the refrigerator for a few hours.

2. Put all the ingredients for the mayonnaise except the rapeseed oil in a beaker or a tall, narrow bowl. Mix, using a hand-held blender, until everything is blended. Put the hand-held blender to the bottom of the bowl and add the rapeseed oil in a thin stream while mixing (hold the hand-held blender still at the bottom of the bowl). When you notice the mayonnaise starting to settle, pull the hand-held blender upwards. Continue mixing to a good consistency.

3. Light the charcoal in the barbecue grill and let it take on a steady, fine glow. Grill the mushroom skewers until they have a nice colour and surface. Then apply indirect heat to the skewers in the grill and roast them for about another 10 minutes.

4. Cut the baguettes in half and rapidly grill them cut-side down. Spread a tablespoon of mayonnaise on each slice of bread and sprinkle the spring onion haulm powder on top. Then lay a mushroom skewer on the sandwich and remove the skewer from the mushrooms.

FRYING PAN BREAD WITH CARAMELISED ONION AND BARBECUE-GRILLED **SHIITAKE MUSHROOMS**

SERVES 6

300 g (10½ oz) shiitake
   mushrooms
3 tablespoons rapeseed
   (canola) oil
salt and black pepper

FOR THE CARAMELISED
ONION
4 medium yellow onions
2 tablespoons rapeseed
   (canola) oil
1 tablespoon apple cider vinegar

FOR THE FRYING PAN BREAD
200–250 ml (7–8 fl oz/scant
   1 cup) plant-based yoghurt
230 g (8 oz/2 cups) strong bread
   flour
2 teaspoons baking powder
½ teaspoon salt
2 tablespoons honey
2 tablespoons rapeseed
   (canola) oil

FOR SERVING
green salad, preferably puntarelle
   chicory (endive)
radish sprouts
salt and black pepper

1. Begin with the caramelised onion. Peel the onions and slice finely. Place in a cold saucepan, add the oil and put the pan on a medium heat. Stir with a wooden spoon once every 5 minutes for 30–40 minutes. Take care to ensure that it doesn't catch and burn. (If you notice that it is getting dry, you can add the vinegar earlier.) Remove the lid, add the vinegar, raise the heat and reduce vigorously for about 15 minutes, stirring continuously. Set the saucepan aside.

2. Continue with the bread. Bring out the yoghurt well in advance to ensure it reaches room temperature. Mix the flour, baking powder and salt in a mixing bowl. Mix the honey and oil with 200 ml (7 fl oz/ scant 1 cup) of yoghurt and add this to the mixing bowl. Quickly work together into a smooth dough, adding more yoghurt if necessary. Roll the dough into a sausage and cut into 6 equally sized pieces. Roll each piece into a thin disc and fry in a hot, dry frying pan (skillet) for about 2 minutes on each side.

3. Clean the shiitake and cut any larger mushrooms to ensure that all pieces are about the same size. Place them in a bowl together with 2 tablespoons of the oil and a little salt and pepper. Mix to ensure they are properly covered. Place the mushrooms in a coarse-meshed strainer and put this on the barbecue grill or hold it over the glow. Occasionally shake the strainer and drip over a little extra oil. The mushrooms are ready when they are a beautiful golden brown.

4. Spread a generous layer of caramelised onion on each piece of bread and top with salad, shiitake, radish sprouts and a little salt and pepper.

BARBECUE-GRILLED **OYSTER MUSHROOMS** WITH BABA GHANOUSH AND POINTED CABBAGE HEARTS

600 g (1 lb 5 oz) pointed
   cabbage, halved
600 g (1 lb 5 oz) oyster
   mushrooms
juice of ½ lemon
salt and black pepper
skewers (soaked for 30 minutes
   if wooden)

FOR THE BABA GHANOUSH
2 medium aubergines (eggplants),
   about 600 g (1 lb 5 oz)
2 garlic cloves, with skin on
juice of ½ lemon
1 teaspoon mild chilli powder,
   such as Espelette peppers
100 ml (3½ fl oz/scant ½ cup)
   olive oil
sea salt flakes

FOR SERVING
olive oil
basil leaves
thyme
spice mix (page 17)
mild chilli powder, such as
   Espelette peppers

1. Light the charcoal in the barbecue and then begin with the baba ghanoush. Pierce the aubergines in a few places using a cocktail stick (tooth pick) and then place them straight onto the glowing charcoal in the barbecue, even if the charcoal is still burning. Grill the aubergines for around 15 minutes until the skin has charred completely and the aubergine is soft inside. Add the garlic when there is 5–10 minutes left and grill them until they are also soft inside. Leave the garlic and aubergine until cool enough to handle.

2. Cut the aubergines lengthways and remove as much flesh as possible with a spoon. Halve the garlic and scoop out the flesh. Place the garlic and aubergine flesh into a large mixing bowl. Add the lemon juice, chilli powder and a little of the oil, and mix using a whisk. Add the rest of the oil, a little at a time, while mixing vigorously. If you prefer a firmer consistency, reduce the amount of oil used. Season with salt.

3. Now that there is a good, even glow to the charcoal, grill the pointed cabbage cut-side down for about 10 minutes until the surface is slightly blackened. Turn it over and place it on the cooler part of the barbecue, leaving it to roast for a while with the lid closed.

4. Thread the oyster mushrooms onto skewers and grill them under pressure by pressing them down with something heavy – I usually use a cast-iron pan. Leave them like this on each side for 5–10 minutes, checking occasionally to ensure they do not burn. They should take on a beautiful, golden brown colour. Then move them to the cooler part of the grill together with the pointed cabbage, squeeze the lemon juice over them, season with salt and pepper and let them roast on the grill under the lid.

5. Add a generous dollop of baba ghanoush to each plate, drizzle a little olive oil over it and plate the pointed cabbage and mushroom skewers. Top with basil, thyme, spice mix and chilli powder.

RYE BREAD WITH GRILLED, SMOKED **PORTOBELLO MUSHROOMS** AND CARAMELISED SHALLOTS

SERVES 6

6 large portobello mushrooms
smoker chips, preferably from
    a fruit tree

FOR THE MARINADE
330 ml (11¼ fl oz/1⅓ cups) beer,
    such as brown ale
2 garlic cloves, lightly crushed
2 tablespoons malt vinegar
1 sprig of rosemary

FOR THE CARAMELISED
SHALLOTS
4 medium shallots
2 tablespoons rapeseed
    (canola) oil
1 tablespoon red wine vinegar

FOR SERVING
12 slices of rye bread
chives, finely sliced
parsley
green mild chilli, finely sliced
sea salt flakes
sriracha mayonnaise
    (page 167)

1. Cut the portobello mushrooms into 1 cm (¾ in) thick slices. Mix the ingredients for the marinade in a plastic bag and then add the sliced mushrooms. Rub the mushrooms through the bag so that the marinade is evenly distributed. Leave to rest in the refrigerator for 7–8 hours. Take it out a few times and rub the portobello mushrooms or shake the bag.

2. Peel and finely slice the shallots. Place in a cold saucepan, add the oil and put the pan on a medium heat. Stir using a wooden spoon once every 5 minutes for 30–40 minutes. Take care to ensure that the mixture does not catch and burn. (If you notice that it is getting dry, you can add the vinegar earlier.) Remove the lid and add the vinegar. Raise the heat and reduce vigorously for about 15 minutes, stirring continuously. Set the saucepan aside.

3. Light the charcoal in the grill and let it take on a steady, fine glow. Take the portobello slices out of the marinade. Place them on paper towels and pat the cut edges dry. Grill the mushrooms until they have a nice colour and surface.

4. Place the mushrooms and shallots on a barbecue-safe plate and set this on the grill. Add some smoker chips to the charcoal and close the barbecue lid to lightly smoke the mushrooms and onions for about 10 minutes.

5. Toast or grill the slices of bread, add a generous dollop of shallot and a few pieces of portobello to each slice. Top with herbs, chilli and a pinch of salt flakes. Serve with mayonnaise on the side.

DEEP-FRIED MUSHROOMS

Slice mushrooms thinly and fry them into the most delicious crisps, or batter them so they retain their soft texture inside: deep-frying is so incredibly tasty and takes the nuttiness of mushrooms to the next dimension. It's best to use a good quality enamel casserole dish if you have one – I've tried deep-frying in all sorts of pots and pans but the result is never quite as good as it is when I use one of these. An enamel casserole dish is not only thick-bottomed, but the enamelled sides provide insulation and help to retain plenty of heat. I've also discovered that peanut (groundnut) oil offers a superior frying experience thanks to its capacity to remain at high temperatures, its neutral flavour and the fact that it can be reused more times than most other oils I have tried out.

05

BEER-BATTERED FRIED **MUSHROOMS** ON A CRISPY SALAD

SERVES 6

600 g (1 lb 5 oz) small mushrooms
200 ml (7 fl oz/scant 1 cup)
    mayonnaise (page 167)
peanut (groundnut) or other frying
    oil
salt

FOR THE SESAME
AND CHILLI SAUCE
1 tablespoon rapeseed
    (canola) oil
1 tablespoon sesame oil
1 tablespoon chilli oil
2 teaspoons apple cider vinegar
1½ teaspoons tahini
1 teaspoon maple syrup

FOR THE BEER BATTER
100 g (3½ oz/scant 1 cup)
    cornflour (cornstarch)
75 g (2½ oz/scant ⅔ cup) plain
    (all-purpose) flour
1 tablespoon rice flour
2 teaspoons baking powder
½ teaspoon salt
200 ml (7 fl oz/scant 1 cup) beer,
    lager or brown ale

FOR SERVING
3 heads of mini romaine lettuce
coriander (cilantro) leaves

1. Place all the ingredients for the sesame and chilli sauce in a bowl and whisk gently with a fork. Set to one side for now.

2. Make the beer batter. Mix the cornflour, plain flour, rice flour, baking powder and salt in a mixing bowl. Then add the beer to the flour mixture and mix into a smooth batter.

3. Put the mushrooms in a bowl with the mayonnaise and stir with a spoon to ensure everything is covered.

4. Heat plenty of frying oil in a high-sided pan until the oil reaches a temperature of about 180°C (350°F). Dip the mushrooms in the beer batter and then place them immediately into the frying oil and fry until they are golden brown. Do this in batches so the oil remains hot. Gently stir them using a slotted spoon while they are frying. Remove the mushrooms, allow excess oil to drain onto a paper towel and then season with salt.

5. Slice the lettuce finely, plate it and top with coriander. Serve the deep-fried mushrooms with sauce on the side.

DEEP-FRIED **MUSHROOM** BALLS IN SALAD LEAVES WITH SMOKY CHILLI SAUCE

FOR THE MUSHROOM BALLS
3 shallots
750 g (1 lb 10 oz) mushrooms
300 g (10½ oz/generous
   1½ cups) cooked arborio rice
60 g (2 oz/1 cup) panko
   breadcrumbs
3 tablespoons cashew butter
   (page 167)
peanut (groundnut) or other frying
   oil
salt (optional)

FOR THE SPICE MIX
2 teaspoons gochugaru (mild
   Korean chilli)
1 tablespoon nutritional yeast
2 teaspoons toasted white sesame
   seeds
2 teaspoons sunflower seeds
1 teaspoon sea salt flakes
1 tablespoon puffed quinoa

FOR SERVING
2 heads of mini romaine lettuce
2 spring onions (scallions)
coriander (cilantro) leaves
black spice mix (page 172)
Midsummer Louisiana sauce
   (page 157)

1. Peel and finely chop the shallots and dice the mushrooms into 5 mm (¾ in) cubes. Heat the oil in a frying pan (skillet) on a high heat until it begins to smoke. Add the shallots and mushrooms and fry on a high heat for about 10–15 minutes until they take on colour. Remove the frying pan from the heat and leave to cool.

2. Mix the rice, panko breadcrumbs and cashew butter in a food processor and mix until fairly smooth in consistency. Place in a mixing bowl and add the mushroom and onion mix. Season with a little salt.

3. Shape the mixture into even-sized balls. Place on a plate and cover with cling film (plastic wrap). Leave them to stand in the refrigerator for at least an hour – preferably longer – so that they hold together better when being deep-fried.

4. Add all the ingredients for the spice mix, except the puffed quinoa, to a food processor and pulse until it is well mixed. Pour the mixture into a bowl, add the puffed quinoa and stir.

5. Heat plenty of frying oil in a high-sided pan until the oil reaches a temperature of about 180°C (350°F). Working in batches, add the mushroom balls and fry until they are golden brown. Gently stir them using a slotted spoon while they are frying. Remove the balls and allow any excess oil to drain onto a paper towel. Sprinkle with a little salt.

6. Serve with the salad leaves, finely sliced spring onions, coriander leaves, a few pinches of spice mix and chilli sauce.

SALAD WITH **KING OYSTER MUSHROOM** CRISPS, CHILLI AND CASHEWS

SERVES 6

FOR THE SALAD
3 heads of mini romaine lettuce
2 red chillies
2 spring onions (scallions)
100 g (3½ oz/⅔ cup) cashews
watercress

FOR THE KING OYSTER
CRISPS
2–3 king oyster mushrooms
groundnut (peanut) or other
    frying oil
salt

FOR THE SAUCE
4 tablespoons Japanese soy
    sauce
2 tablespoons vinegar (12%)
2 teaspoons sesame oil
1 teaspoon Sichuan pepper oil

1. Slice the lettuce, chillies and spring onions finely. Crush the nuts, either in a food processor or using a pestle and mortar.

2. Slice the mushrooms finely. Heat plenty of frying oil in a high-sided pan until the oil reaches a temperature of about 180°C (350°F). Add the mushroom slices and fry until they are golden brown. Gently stir them using a slotted spoon while they are frying. Remove the mushroom crisps and allow any excess oil to drain onto a paper towel. Sprinkle with salt on both sides.

3. In a bowl, whisk together the soy sauce, vinegar and sesame oil. Drizzle with Sichuan pepper oil.

4. Mix the lettuce, spring onions and mushroom crisps (chips) with your hands. Top with the chillies and nuts. Serve with the sauce on the side.

DEEP-FRIED **KING OYSTER MUSHROOMS** AND SWEET POTATO NOODLES IN CORIANDER BROTH

SERVES 6

FOR THE KING OYSTER
MUSHROOM CRISPS
2–3 king oyster mushrooms
peanut (groundnut) or other
    frying oil
salt

FOR THE SHOJIN DASHI
WITH CORIANDER BROTH
1 litre (34 fl oz/4 cups) shojin
    dashi (page 161)
2 cm (¾ in) ginger root, sliced
1 cinnamon stick
1 star anise
1 teaspoon black pepper
1 teaspoon coriander seeds
1 teaspoon Sichuan peppercorns
2 tablespoons rice vinegar
1 pot of coriander (cilantro)
salt

FOR SERVING
300 g (10½ oz) sweet potato
    noodles
spring onions (scallions), finely
    chopped
3 teaspoons sesame oil
sunflower sprouts
radish sprouts

1. Begin with the broth. Bring the dashi to the boil together with everything except the rice vinegar, fresh coriander and salt. Boil for around 15 minutes. Take off the heat. Add the vinegar and then the coriander. Stir a few times, cover with the lid and leave to stand for around 20 minutes. Strain and season with a little salt.

2. Slice the mushrooms thinly. Heat plenty of frying oil in a high-sided pan until the oil reaches a temperature of about 180°C (350°F). Add the mushroom slices and fry until they are golden brown. Gently stir them using a slotted spoon while they are frying. Remove the mushroom crisps (chips) and allow any excess oil to drain onto a paper towel. Season with salt on both sides.

3. Add water to a pan and bring to the boil. Add the noodles, then set the pan to one side. Leave them to stand for 3–5 minutes, then drain them when they feel tender.

4. Serve the noodles in deep dishes and pour a little warm broth over them. Top with the king oyster mushroom crisps, spring onions, a few drops of sesame oil and sunflower and radish sprouts.

Photo caption: Deep-Fried King Oyster Mushrooms, Kale and Carrots in Broth with Butter Beans (page 118)

DEEP-FRIED MUSHROOMS

DEEP-FRIED **KING OYSTER MUSHROOMS,** KALE AND CARROTS IN BROTH WITH BUTTER BEANS

SERVES 6

300 g (10½ oz) king oyster mushrooms
3 carrots
150 g (5 oz) kale
peanut (groundnut) or other frying oil
salt

FOR THE BROTH
1.2 litres (40 fl oz/4¾ cups) shojin
   dashi (page 161)
3 garlic cloves, lightly crushed
1 teaspoon black pepper
1 teaspoon coriander seeds
1 teaspoon Sichuan pepper
2 teaspoons tamari
2 teaspoons sherry vinegar
40 g (1½ oz) chervil
300 g (10½ oz) cooked butter (lima)
   beans

FOR THE SOY, MISO AND
HAZELNUT MAYONNAISE
100 ml (3½ fl oz/scant ½ cup)
   aquafaba
2 teaspoons tamari
1 tablespoon miso
2 tablespoons hazelnut butter
1 tablespoon sherry vinegar
1 pinch of black pepper
500 ml (17 fl oz/2 cups) rapeseed
   (canola) oil (not cold pressed)

FOR SERVING
chervil
chilli oil

1. Make the broth. Bring the dashi to the boil together with the garlic, black pepper, coriander seeds, Sichuan pepper and tamari. Boil for 15 minutes. Remove from the heat, add the vinegar and chervil. Stir a few times, cover with the lid and leave to stand for around 20 minutes. Strain and bring the broth back to the boil. Add the beans and simmer for 10 minutes.

2. Put all the ingredients for the mayonnaise, except the rapeseed oil, into a tall, narrow bowl. Blend uing a hand-held blender. Put the blender to the bottom of the bowl and add the rapeseed oil in a thin stream while mixing. When you notice the mayonnaise starting to settle, pull the blender upwards. Continue mixing to a good consistency.

3. Cut the mushrooms into slices about 3 mm (⅛ in) thick. Peel the carrots and cut into thin slices, preferably using a mandoline. Cut off the stem of the kale.

4. Heat plenty of frying oil in a high-sided pan until the oil reaches a temperature of about 180°C (350°F). Add the mushroom slices and fry until they are golden brown. Gently stir them using a slotted spoon while they are frying. Remove the mushrooms and allow any excess oil to drain onto a paper towel. Season with salt. Continue with the carrot slices and then the kale. When it is time to fry the kale, a temperature of around 140°C (275°F) is ideal to avoid them burning. Place the carrots and kale on a paper towel and season with salt.

5. Place the carrots and kale into bowls and then add the broth and beans. Top with mushrooms, chervil, chilli oil and a dollop of the mayonnaise.

DEEP-FRIED **NAMEKO AND KING OYSTER MUSHROOMS** WITH ROASTED KALE IN A SHERRY AND MUSHROOM BROTH

SERVES 6

SERVES 6

FOR THE SHERRY AND
MUSHROOM BROTH

2 medium onions

1 teaspoon black pepper

1 teaspoon coriander seeds

1 teaspoon Sichuan pepper

1.3 litres (45 fl oz/4⅓ cups) roasted
    mushroom broth (page 160)

200 ml (7 fl oz/scant 1 cup) sherry

1 tablespoon sherry vinegar

2–3 sprigs of parsley

sea salt

FOR THE ROASTED KALE

200 g (7 oz) kale

2 garlic cloves

2 tablespoons cooking oil

sea salt flakes and black pepper

FOR THE DEEP-FRIED
NAMEKO AND KING OYSTER
MUSHROOMS

2 king oyster mushrooms

150 g (5 oz) nameko mushrooms

peanut (groundnut) or other frying oil

salt

FOR SERVING

bean sprouts

spring onions (scallions), finely chopped

serrano chilli, finely sliced

3 teaspoons avocado oil

1. Begin with the broth. Cut the onions in half and burn the cut edges in a really hot, dry frying pan (skillet). Add the onions, black pepper, coriander seeds and Sichuan pepper to the mushroom broth and sherry. (Feel free to toast your spices first for a deeper flavour.) Bring to the boil and then leave to simmer for around 1 hour.

2. Remove the pan from the heat. Add the sherry vinegar and then the parsley. Stir a few times, cover with the lid and leave to stand for 20 minutes. Strain and season with a little salt.

3. Heat the oven to 120°C (250°F/gas 1). Cut off the stem of the kale if it is thick and woody. Place the kale and garlic cloves in a baking tray (pan) and drizzle with the oil. Season with salt and pepper. Roast the cabbage in the middle of the oven for 20–25 minutes. Remove from the oven and place on a rack.

4. Finely slice the king oyster mushrooms. Heat plenty of frying oil in a high-sided pan until the oil reaches a temperature of about 180°C (350°F). Add the mushroom slices and nameko mushrooms and fry until they are golden brown. Gently stir them using a slotted spoon while they are frying. Remove the mushrooms and allow any excess oil to drain onto a paper towel. Lightly salt.

5. Add a heap of kale to each bowl before adding some warm broth to each. Top with the deep-fried nameko and king oyster mushrooms, bean sprouts, spring onions, chilli and a bit of avocado oil.

DEEP-FRIED MUSHROOMS

PICKLED MUSHROOMS

Marinating, pickling or preserving mushrooms is great for all manner of reasons. Back in the day, the main aim was to preserve food. But for me, it is mostly about experimenting with additional flavours and achieving the perfect balance between texture and other ingredients in any dish. Mind you, it's no bad thing that the mushrooms also keep for longer and that you have them standing by in your refrigerator or larder.

So feel free to increase the quantity of marinated, pickled or preserved mushrooms that you prepare when using these recipes so that you have a great flavour-maker easily accessible for the foreseeable future.

06

COLD CUCUMBER SOUP WITH SICHUAN PEPPER, SESAME AND SOY-PICKLED **SHIITAKE MUSHROOMS**

SERVES 6

300 g (10½ oz) shiitake mushrooms
2 tablespoons rapeseed (canola) oil
1 teaspoon sesame oil
2 cucumbers
300 g (10½ oz) ramen noodles from
    SLURP (page 164)

FOR THE MARINADE
1 teaspoon black pepper
1 teaspoon coriander seeds
1 teaspoon Sichuan pepper
4 tablespoons lightly salted soy sauce
1 tablespoon shio koji
1 tablespoon mirin, preferably hon mirin
2 bird's eye chillies
1 tablespoon cane sugar or caster
    (superfine) sugar
2 garlic cloves
2 teaspoons sesame oil

FOR THE COLD CUCUMBER SOUP
2 cucumbers
800 ml (28 fl oz/3½ cups) shojin dashi
    (page 161)
1 tablespoon shio koji
1 tablespoon mirin, preferably
    hon mirin
salt

FOR SERVING
bean sprouts
Sichuan pepper oil

1. Begin with the marinade, preferably a few hours prior to serving. Heat a cast-iron pan on a medium heat. Toast the black pepper, coriander seeds and Sichuan pepper until the seeds turn golden brown and you can clearly smell the spices. Using a mortar and pestle, crush them finely. Save around 1 teaspoon for serving and pour the remainder into a food processor along with all other ingredients for the marinade. Blend until smooth.

2. Clean and prepare the mushrooms before cutting into slices 1 cm (¾ in) thick. Heat the oil in a frying pan (skillet) on a high heat until it begins to smoke. Add the mushrooms and fry on a high heat for about 5 minutes until they begin to colour. Remove the frying pan from the heat and allow it to cool. Add the marinade and stir a few times. Pour the mixture into a bowl, wrap in cling film (plastic wrap) and leave in the refrigerator for a few hours.

3. Peel the cucumbers, then cut the flesh into 5 mm (¼ in) dice, discarding the seeds. Set to one side for now. Put the cucumber peel into a food processor, add the other ingredients for the soup and mix finely.

4. Add plenty of water to a pan and bring to the boil. Add the noodles and leave them for 40 seconds. Strain under cold running water.

5. Strain the marinade from the mushrooms. Put the noodles into deep plates, add a little of the cold cucumber soup, top with bean sprouts, the diced cucumber, mushrooms, a few drops of Sichuan pepper oil and a little of the reserved pepper spice.

PICKLED **MUSHROOMS** WITH GREEN PEA HUMMUS AND GREEN DUKKAH

SERVES 6

600 g (1 lb 5 oz) mushrooms

FOR THE MARINADE
2–3 coriander (cilantro) roots
½ teaspoon black pepper
½ teaspoon coriander seeds
1 teaspoon cayenne pepper
1 teaspoon whole cumin
½ teaspoon salt
1 tablespoon date syrup
1 tablespoon lime juice
1 tablespoon vinegar
2 garlic cloves
1 tablespoon olive oil
2 teaspoons sesame oil

FOR THE PISTACHIO DUKKAH
225 g (8 oz) pistachios, shelled
1 teaspoon coriander seeds
½ teaspoon cumin seeds
1 teaspoon cayenne pepper
½ teaspoon dried oregano
1 teaspoon salt
zest of 1 lime

FOR THE GREEN PEA HUMMUS
300 g (10½ oz) cooked green peas
440 g (15 oz) cooked chickpeas
100 ml (3½ fl oz) olive oil
1 tablespoon tahini
1 garlic clove
juice of ½ lime
3 tablespoons finely chopped mint
salt

FOR SERVING
green chilli, finely sliced
kale sprouts
coriander (cilantro)

1. Prepare the marinade, preferably a few hours prior to serving. Begin by finely chopping the coriander roots. Using a mortar and pestle, crush them along with the black pepper and coriander seeds. Combine with the other ingredients for the marinade in a food processor and mix until smooth.

2. Clean and prepare the mushrooms before cutting them into quarters. Heat some oil in a frying pan (skillet) on a high heat until it begins to smoke. Add the mushrooms and fry on a high heat until they begin to colour, for about 5 minutes. Remove the frying pan from the heat, add the marinade and stir a few times to ensure that all the mushrooms are covered. Pour the mixture into a bowl, wrap in cling film (plastic wrap) and leave in the refrigerator for a few hours.

3. Make the dukkah. Put a dry frying pan on a medium heat and add the nuts and coriander seeds. Toast for about 5 minutes until they colour. Stir occasionally to ensure they do not burn. Place in a food processor and add the cumin, cayenne pepper, oregano and salt. Run a few blitzes or pulses – it should be in small chunks but not too finely chopped. Finish by adding the lime zest.

4. Using a food processor or hand-held blender, mix all the ingredients for the pea hummus until smooth. If you prefer a slightly coarser hummus, you can add the peas last and then mix using just a few pulses.

5. Fill half of each bowl with hummus and fill the remaining half with mushrooms. Top with chilli, kale sprouts, coriander and the dukkah.

MARINATED **SHIITAKE MUSHROOMS** ON DEEP-FRIED RICE PAPER

SERVES 6

300 g (10½ oz) shiitake
   mushrooms
2 tablespoons rapeseed (canola)
   oil, plus about 1 litre (34 fl oz/
   4 cups) for deep-frying
6 round rice papers

FOR THE MARINADE
2–3 coriander (cilantro) roots
   (page 55)
2 lemongrass stalks
4 tablespoons lightly salted soy
   sauce
2 tablespoons lime juice
2 teaspoons dark miso
2 teaspoons sesame oil
1 tablespoon cane sugar or caster
   (superfine) sugar

FOR SERVING
sunflower sprouts
radish sprouts
mint
chilli, such as prik chee fah chilli
   from Thailand, finely chopped

1. Prepare the marinade, preferably a few hours prior to serving. Begin by finely chopping the coriander roots. Split the lemongrass in half and remove the purple inner part and finely chop it. Combine this with the other ingredients for the marinade in a food processor and mix until smooth.

2. Clean and prepare the mushrooms. Heat the oil in a frying pan (skillet) on a high heat until it begins to smoke. Add the mushrooms and fry on a high heat for about 5 minutes until they begin to colour. Add the marinade and stir a few times to ensure that all the mushrooms are covered. Pour the mixture into a bowl, wrap in cling film (plastic wrap) and leave in the refrigerator for a few hours.

3. Heat plenty of frying oil in a high-sided pan until the oil reaches a temperature of about 180°C (350°F). Add the rice paper and fry for a few seconds. They cook quickly and it is clearly visible when they are puffed and done. Remove the rice puffs and allow any excess oil to drain onto a paper towel.

4. Strain the marinade from the mushrooms. Break a puffed rice paper in the middle, add some mushrooms and top with sunflower and radish sprouts, mint and chilli.

Tip: Save the marinade and reuse it for marinating something else, such as dried king oyster mushrooms (page 152).

FRIED KIMCHI AND MARINATED **SHIITAKE MUSHROOMS** WITH CORIANDER AND MUSHROOM BROTH

SERVES 6

300 g (10½ oz) shiitake
    mushrooms
600 g (12 lb 5 oz) kimchi
3 tablespoons peanut (groundnut)
    oil or rapeseed (canola) oil

FOR THE MARINADE
juice of the kimchi
4 tablespoons shoyu soy
2 teaspoons sesame oil
1 tablespoon vinegar (12%)
1 tablespoon agave syrup

FOR THE CORIANDER AND
MUSHROOM BROTH
1 litre (34 fl oz/4 cups) roasted
    mushroom broth (page 160)
2 lemongrass stalks, split in half
3 garlic cloves, lightly crushed
1 teaspoon black pepper
1 teaspoon coriander seeds
1 teaspoon Sichuan peppercorns
3 teaspoons sesame oil
2 tablespoons rice vinegar
1 pot of fresh coriander (cilantro)
salt

FOR SERVING
coriander (cilantro) leaves
radish sprouts

1. Start by marinating the shiitake. A few hours before serving, strain and squeeze the liquid from the kimchi into a bowl. Set the kimchi aside and mix the juice with the other ingredients for the marinade in a bag. Seal the bag and place in the refrigerator for a few hours, turning the bag every now and then.

2. Put the mushroom broth, lemongrass, garlic, black pepper, coriander seeds and Sichuan peppercorns in a pan and bring to the boil. Boil for around 15 minutes. Remove from the heat, then add the sesame oil, vinegar and coriander. Stir a few times, cover with the lid and leave to stand for around 20 minutes. Strain and season with a little salt.

3. Strain the marinade from the mushrooms. Heat the oil in a frying pan (skillet) on a high heat until it begins to smoke. Add the kimchi and fry on a high heat for about 5 minutes until it begins to colour. Add the mushrooms and then lower the heat to medium. Leave to simmer for about 10 minutes, stirring occasionally.

4. Place a generous heap of the kimchi and shiitake mix into each bowl. Top up with some broth before finishing with coriander and radish sprouts.

Tip: Save the marinade and reuse it for marinating something else, such as the mushroom jerky (page 152).

MARINATED **PORTOBELLO MUSHROOM** WITH RADICCHIO, ASPARAGUS AND SESAME SAUCE

600 g (1 lb 5 oz) portobello
   mushrooms
1 tablespoon oil
250 g (9 oz) asparagus
300 g (10½ oz) radicchio

FOR THE MARINADE
2–3 coriander (cilantro) roots
   (page 55)
1 onion
½ teaspoon black pepper
½ teaspoon coriander seeds
½ teaspoon Sichuan peppercorns
1 tablespoon cane sugar or caster
   (superfine) sugar
4 tablespoons lightly salted soy
   sauce
2 tablespoons vinegar (12%)
2 bird's eye chillies
2 teaspoons grated ginger root
2 garlic cloves
2 teaspoons sesame oil

FOR THE SESAME SAUCE
1 tablespoon mayonnaise
1 tablespoon mild chilli sauce
2 teaspoon soy sauce
1½ teaspoons tahini
1 teaspoon mirin
1 teaspoon sesame oil
1 teaspoon maple syrup

FOR SERVING
green chilli, finely chopped
coriander (cilantro) leaves

1. Marinate the portobello mushrooms, preferably a few hours prior to serving. Begin by finely chopping the coriander roots. Using a mortar and pestle, crush the onion, black pepper, coriander seeds and Sichuan pepper. (Feel free to toast your spices first for a deeper flavour.) Combine with the other ingredients for the marinade in a food processor and mix until smooth. Or continue using your mortar and pestle if you have a large set.

2. Clean and prepare the mushrooms before cutting into slices 1 cm (½ in) thick. Heat some of the oil in a frying pan (skillet) on a high heat until it begins to smoke. Add the mushrooms and fry on a high heat until they begin to colour, for about 5 minutes. Remove the frying pan from the heat and add the marinade. Stir a few times to ensure that all the mushrooms are covered. Pour the mixture into a bowl, wrap in cling film (plastic wrap) and leave in the refrigerator for a few hours.

3. Remove the tips of the asparagus and slice the rest. Give your frying pan a wipe and return to a medium heat. Add the remaining oil and gently fry the asparagus, tossing them from time to time. The intention is not for them to take colour but to make them soft and tender while retaining a raw core.

4. Place all the ingredients for the sesame sauce in a bowl and whisk gently with a fork.

5. Strain the marinade from the mushrooms. Break whole leaves off the radicchio and place on each plate, spoon generous helpings of asparagus on top and drizzle with the sesame sauce. Top with chilli, coriander and the marinated portobello mushrooms. Eat with chopsticks or fold the radicchio leaves and eat with your hands.

DRIED MUSHROOMS

Drying mushrooms is straightforward and useful in many different ways. First and foremost, the process concentrates the flavours in the mushrooms, transforming them into umami bombs that are great for flavouring everything from broths to sauces and stews that are either left to cook for a long time or need a final boost towards the end. They are also great for taking away among your provisions – whether you are off for a day trip or on a longer holiday – where you want to pack lightly and will keep them at room temperature. Dried mushrooms keep for years if they are kept in the dark. I usually cut the mushrooms into slices of about 5 mm (¼ in) thick and dry them at a temperature of about 50°C (125°F/ gas low) in the oven, or at the even lower temperature of 35°C (95°F) over a longer period if you have a specialist drying oven. Bear in mind that dried mushrooms often need to be left to soak if they are being used for any purpose except as a dry seasoning, so read the recipe carefully!

07

MUSHROOMS

PORCINI MUSHROOM RISOTTO
WITH CASHEW BUTTER

SERVES 6

4 tablespoons cashew butter
  (page 167)
3 tablespoons olive oil, plus extra
  to drizzle
1 litre (34 fl oz/4 cups) water

FOR THE RISOTTO MIX
40 g (1½ oz) dried porcini
  mushrooms
385 g (13 oz/1¾ cups) arborio
  rice
30 g (1 oz) dried onion
2 teaspoons dried parsley
2 teaspoons dried wild garlic
1 tablespoon stock powder
1 teaspoon salt

FOR THE SPICE MIX
1 teaspoon dried lovage
1 tablespoon nutritional yeast
1 teaspoon dried lemon zest
½ teaspoon black peppercorns
½ teaspoon coriander seeds
½ teaspoon Sichuan peppercorns
1 teaspoon sea salt

1. Mix together all the ingredients for the risotto mix. Crush the spices for the spice mix using a pestle and mortar. Then add the cashew butter, olive oil and risotto and spice mixes to separate containers (see the illustration on page 136).

2. Heat the oil in a frying pan (skillet) over a medium heat. Add the risotto mix and fry for about 10 minutes until the rice is glossy, stirring occasionally to ensure it does not burn. Lower the heat, add the cashew butter and stir. Add 700 ml (24 fl oz/scant 3 cups) of the water and season with some of the spice mix. Boil for 15–20 minutes. Add more water occasionally as it cooks, about 100 ml (3½ fl oz/scant ½ cup) every 5 minutes.

3. Place a generous portion of risotto on each plate, drizzle with a little olive oil and top with the spice mix according to taste.

DRIED **CHANTERELLE MUSHROOMS** WITH SWEET POTATO NOODLES, TOOTHED WRACK AND BROTH

SERVES 6

1 litre (34 fl oz/4 cups) water
30 g (1 oz) dried chanterelle
    mushrooms
30 g (1 oz) dried onion
10 g (½ oz) dried toothed wrack
    or nori
2 tablespoons rapeseed (canola)
    oil
500 g (1 lb 2 oz) sweet potato
    noodles

FOR THE FURIKAKE
1 tablespoon whole buckwheat
1 tablespoon sunflower seeds
2 teaspoons black sesame seeds
2 teaspoons white sesame seeds
½ teaspoon Sichuan peppercorns
10 g (½ oz) dried dead man's
    fingers or dried nori
½ teaspoon sea salt

FOR THE SAUCE
100 ml (3½ fl oz/scant ½ cup) sake
1 tablespoon shio koji
1 tablespoon mirin
1 tablespoon Japanese soy sauce
2 teaspoons sesame oil
10 g (½ oz) vegetable stock powder
½ teaspoon salt

1. Begin with the furikake. Put a dry frying pan (skillet) on a medium heat and add the buckwheat, sunflower seeds, sesame seeds and Sichuan peppercorns. Toast for around 5 minutes until everything begins to colour and smells fragrant. Stir occasionally to ensure it does not burn. Remove from the heat and leave to cool. Put everything in a food processor, break down the seaweed and add to the processor with the salt. Run a few blitzes or pulses – it should be in small chunks but not too finely chopped. Store in a dry, airtight container.

2. Bring the water to the boil in a large saucepan, then remove from the heat and add the dried mushrooms, onion and seaweed. Cover with the lid and leave to stand for around 15 minutes. Strain the liquid into a saucepan, squeeze and dry off any surplus liquid from the mushrooms and onion and set aside. Separately, set the seaweed aside.

3. Mix all the ingredients for the sauce in a bowl. Heat the oil in a frying pan on a high heat until it begins to smoke. Add the mushroom mixture and fry for around 10 minutes, stirring occasionally to ensure it does not burn. Lower the heat, add the sauce and cook for a further 10 minutes.

4. Bring the liquid for soaking the mushrooms back to the boil and add the noodles. Stir and cook for 6 minutes until they are soft.

5. Serve the noodles and seaweed in deep dishes and pour a little warm broth over them. Top with the mushroom mix and furikake.

DRIED **WOOD EAR MUSHROOMS** WITH NOODLES AND COURGETTES, TOPPED WITH CHILLI SPICE

1 litre (34 fl oz/4 cups) water
40 g (1½ oz) dried wood ear
   mushrooms (available in Asian
   grocery stores)
2 tablespoons rapeseed
   (canola) oil
3 garlic cloves, thinly sliced
6 dried noodle nests
60 g (2 oz) dried courgette
   (zucchini)
1 teaspoon salt

FOR THE CHILLI SPICE MIX
½ teaspoon black pepper
½ teaspoon coriander seeds
1–2 bird's eye chillies
1 teaspoon dried, ground ginger
   root

FOR THE SAUCE
2 tablespoons Japanese soy
   sauce
1 tablespoon apple cider vinegar
2 teaspoons toasted sesame oil

1. Bring the water to the boil in a large saucepan. Remove the saucepan from the heat, add the dried mushrooms, cover with the lid and leave to stand for around 15 minutes.

2. Strain the liquid into a saucepan to use later as a broth, then squeeze and dry off any surplus liquid from the mushrooms. Remove the mushroom stems, which are chewy and dull, and then cut the mushrooms into long strips.

3. Crush all the ingredients for the spice mix using a mortar and pestle. Set to one side.

4. Mix all the ingredients for the sauce together in a bowl.

5. Heat the oil in a frying pan (skillet) on a high heat until it begins to smoke. Add the mushrooms and fry on a high heat for about 10 minutes until they are crispy. Season with a little of the chilli spice mix while frying and then add the garlic. Lower the heat and then add the sauce.

6. Bring the broth back to the boil, add the noodles and courgette and stir. Cook for 7–8 minutes until the noodles are soft.

7. Place the noodles in deep plates. Top with the mushroom strips and season with more of the chilli spice mix and salt.

Dried Wood-Ear Mushrooms with Noodles and Courgettes, topped with Chilli Spice (page 143)

DRIED **CHANTERELLE MUSHROOMS** WITH RIBBON NOODLES, BROTH AND PISTACHIO DUKKAH

SERVES 6

1 litre (34 fl oz/4 cups) water
40 g (1½ oz) dried chanterelle
  mushrooms
60 g (2 oz) dried broccoli
15 g (½ oz) dried onion
2 tablespoons rapeseed
  (canola) oil
900 g (2 lb) ribbon noodles
1 teaspoon salt

FOR THE PISTACHIO DUKKAH
225 g (8 oz/1⅔ cups) shelled
  pistachios
1 teaspoon coriander seeds
½ teaspoon whole cumin
1 teaspoon cayenne pepper
½ teaspoon dried oregano
1 teaspoon salt

FOR THE SAUCE
100 ml (3½ fl oz/scant ½ cup)
  beer
1 tablespoon shio koji
1 tablespoon malt vinegar
2 teaspoons mild chilli oil
2 teaspoons date syrup
10 g (½ oz) vegetable stock
  powder
½ teaspoon salt

1. Begin with the pistachio dukkah. Put a dry frying pan (skillet) on a medium heat and add the nuts and coriander seeds. Toast for about 5 minutes until they colour. Stir occasionally to ensure they do not burn. Take off the heat. Place in a food processor together with the remaining dukkah ingredients. Run a few blitzes or pulses – it should be in small chunks but not too finely chopped.

2. Mix all the ingredients for the sauce and set aside.

3. Bring the water to the boil in a saucepan. Remove from the heat and add the chanterelles, broccoli and onion. Cover with the lid and leave to stand for around 15 minutes.

4. Strain the liquid into a saucepan to use later as a broth, then squeeze and dry off any surplus liquid from the mushrooms and vegetables.

5. Heat the oil in a frying pan (skillet) on a high heat until it begins to smoke. Add the mushroom mixture and fry for around 10 minutes, stirring occasionally to ensure it does not burn. Lower the heat and then add the sauce. Leave to cook for another 10 minutes.

6. Bring the broth back to the boil and add the noodles. Stir and leave to stand for 6 minutes until the noodles are soft.

7. Serve the noodles in deep dishes and pour a little warm broth over them. Top with the fried mushroom mix and dukkah.

DRIED **KING OYSTER MUSHROOMS** WITH KIMCHI AND WHEAT NOODLES

SERVES 6

1 litre (34 fl oz/4 cups) water
40 g (1½ oz) dried king oyster
   mushrooms
60 g (2 oz) dried kimchi
30 g (1 oz) dried leeks
2 tablespoons rapeseed
   (canola) oil
3 tablespoons gochugaru
   (mild Korean chilli)
1 teaspoon salt
6 noodle nests

FOR THE SAUCE
3 tablespoons Japanese soy
   sauce
2 tablespoons mirin, preferably
   hon mirin
1 tablespoon sherry vinegar
2 teaspoons sesame oil
1 teaspoon cane sugar or caster
   (superfine) sugar

1. Bring the water to the boil and then take the saucepan off the heat. Add the mushrooms, kimchi and leeks, cover with the lid and leave to stand for about 15 minutes.

2. Strain the liquid into a saucepan to use later as a broth, then squeeze and dry off any surplus liquid from the mushrooms and vegetables.

4. Mix all the ingredients for the sauce in a bowl.

5. Heat the oil in a frying pan (skillet) on a high heat until it begins to smoke. Add the mushrooms, kimchi and leek and fry on a high heat until everything colours. Season with gochugaru and salt and fry for about 10 minutes. Lower the heat and then add the sauce.

6. Bring the broth back to the boil, add the noodles and stir. Cook for 3–4 minutes until soft.

7. Place the noodles in a deep dish and pour a little of the warm broth over them. Top with the mushrooms and vegetables, and season with a little more gochugaru and salt.

2 X SNACKS: **KING OYSTER MUSHROOM** JERKY POPCORN WITH **MUSHROOM SPICE**

SERVES 6

1.5 kg (3 lb 5 oz) king oyster
   mushrooms
2 tablespoons gochugaru
   (mild Korean chilli)

FOR THE MARINADE
3 coriander (cilantro) roots
   (page 55)
1 teaspoon black pepper
1 teaspoon coriander seeds
1 teaspoon Sichuan pepper
2 tablespoons cane sugar
100 ml (3½ fl oz/scant ½ cup)
   lightly salted soy sauce
1 tablespoon shin mirin
1 tablespoon vinegar (12%)
2 teaspoons sesame oil

SERVES 6

1 tablespoon whole black
   peppercorns
1 tablespoon coriander seeds
1 tablespoon Sichuan peppercorns
100 ml (3½ fl oz/scant ½ cup)
   sea salt
60 g (2 oz) dried porcini
   mushrooms
2–3 tablespoons oil
100 g (3½ oz/½ cup) popcorn
   kernels

King Oyster Mushroom Jerky

1. Begin with the marinade. Finely chop the coriander roots and then crush them using a mortar and pestle along with the black pepper, coriander seeds and Sichuan pepper. Combine with the other ingredients for the marinade in a food processor and mix until smooth.

2. Cut the mushrooms into fine 2–3 mm (⅛ in) thick slices, preferably with a mandoline. Put the mushrooms in a bowl, add the marinade and gochugaru and then stir to ensure that everything is well mixed. Wrap in cling film (plastic wrap) and leave in the refrigerator for a few hours or overnight.

3. Heat the oven to 70°C (160°F/gas low) and line a baking tray (pan) with baking parchment. Remove the mushrooms from the marinade and shake gently to ensure the mushrooms are not too moist. Lay them on the sheet and leave to dry in the oven for about 8 hours. Check on them after a few hours – the time may vary depending on thickness and how much liquid there is around the mushrooms.

Popcorn with Mushroom Spice

1. Heat a cast-iron pan on a medium heat. Toast the black pepper, coriander seeds and Sichuan peppercorns until the seeds turn golden brown.

2. Mix the spices, salt and mushrooms into a fine powder using a spice blender. Shake the spice mixture through a finely meshed sieve.

3. Heat the oil in a large, lidded pan over a medium heat. Add a couple of pieces of popcorn and when they puff up, add the remaining popcorn and put on the lid. After a few minutes when the corn has stopped popping, season immediately with the mushroom spice mix.

IN THE PANTRY

I'm a little obsessed with fermented ingredients such as kimchi, spice mixes like furikake and dukkah, various types of chilli sauce, pastes and nut butters, and it goes without saying that it is way tastier and far more satisfying to make your own instead of buying them ready made. But there are also a few slightly rarer ingredients that can be bought if you know where to look, and I have provided recommendations for those here too.

08

Lacto-fermented shiitake mushrooms

750 g (1 lb 10 oz) shiitake
    mushrooms
15 g (½ oz) salt
1 large sterilised 1 litre (34 fl oz/
    4 cup) preserving jar with a
    rubber seal and bracket lock

// Put the fresh mushrooms in
the freezer for at least 24 hours.
This helps to break down the cell
structure so that the mushrooms
release more flavour during the
fermentation process.
// Take the mushrooms out of the
freezer and leave them to thaw to
room temperature. Put them in a
bowl and sprinkle with salt (equal
to about 2% of the mushrooms'
weight) and leave to stand for
1 hour. Stir occasionally to ensure
that everything is well mixed.
// Put the mushrooms into the
glass jar a little at a time. Gently
apply pressure with a wooden
spoon to make everything fit.
Make sure all the salt is dissolved
in the liquid formed in the bowl,
then add the liquid. Fill a plastic
bag with some water, then knot
the bag and place on top of the
mushrooms as a weight. Close
the lid and seal with the bracket.
// Leave the jar to stand at room
temperature for 5–7 days. Then
leave it in the refrigerator for at
least 1 week to allow the flavours
time to properly develop.

**Tip: This can be eaten as it is,
or used as a flavour enhancer
in dishes such as broths, sauces
and marinades.**

Kimchi base

Makes about 750 g (1 lb 10 oz)

500 ml (17 fl oz/2 cups) water
2 tablespoons rice flour
100 g (3½ oz) light miso
2 silver onions, roughly chopped
2 white or yellow medium carrots,
    coarsely chopped
100 g (3½ oz) radishes, coarsely
    chopped in 3–4 cm (1½ in)
    chunks
about 12 g (½ oz) ginger root
10 garlic cloves, coarsely chopped
250 g (9 oz) mild white chilli, such
    as aji peppers

// Pour the water and rice flour
into a saucepan, bring to the boil,
then simmer for around 5 minutes.
Remove the saucepan from the
heat and allow the mixture to
cool. You can leave it in the
refrigerator overnight.
// Put the onions, carrots, radishes,
ginger and garlic in a food
processor and mix into a fine
purée. If it is too thick, you can
add a dash of water.
// Pour the rice flour mixture, the
vegetable purée and chillies into
a glass jar and mix thoroughly.
Keep in the refrigerator. If you
don't intend to use it for a while,
you can also freeze it.

Kimchi

Makes about 1.2 kg (2 lb 4 oz)

1 kg (2lb 4 oz) Chinese cabbage
100 g (3½ oz) daikon, peeled
100 g (3½ oz) rhubarb stalks
1¼ tablespoons salt
200 ml (7 fl oz) kimchi base
    (see left)
1.5 litre (52 fl oz/6¼ cup) sterilised
    preserving jar with a rubber
    seal and bracket lock

// Cut the Chinese cabbage
lengthways and then cut into slices
1 cm (¾ in) thick. Use as much of
the cabbage as possible.
// Cut the daikon and rhubarb
into thin batons. Put the batons
in a bowl with the cabbage and
massage in the salt. Leave to
stand at room temperature for at
least 1 hour so that the vegetables
have time to release liquid. Occasionally turn over the cabbage
and squeeze. Then add the kimchi
base and stir or massage with
your hands to ensure it is all well
mixed.
// Put the kimchi into the glass jar
a little at a time. Apply pressure
with a wooden spoon to make
everything fit (including the liquid).
Close the lid and seal with the
bracket.
// Place the jar on a plate and
ideally stand it in a plastic bag
since it is very likely that some
liquid will be ejected Leave the jar
to stand at room temperature for
5–7 days. The longer it is left, the
more acidic it will be.
// Leave the jar in the refrigerator
for at least 1 week to allow the
flavours time to develop.

Fermented yellow tomato sauce

Makes about 1 kg (2 lb 4 oz)

1 kg (2 lb 4 oz) yellow tomatoes
100 g (3½ oz) celery stalks
1¼ tablespoons iodine-free salt
200 ml (7 fl oz/scant 1 cup) white
  kimchi base (see left)
1.5 litre (52 fl oz/6¼ cup) sterilised
  preserving jar with a rubber
  seal and bracket lock

// Rinse the tomatoes and halve
them. Clean the celery and slice it
thinly. Put the tomatoes and celery
in a bowl and massage in the
salt. Apply plenty of pressure to
the tomatoes so that they release
liquid. Leave to stand at room
temperature for at least 1 hour. Stir
and apply pressure occasionally.
Then add the kimchi base and stir
or massage with your hands to
ensure it is all well mixed.
// Pour the mixture into the jar but
leave 2–3 cm (1 in) of air at the
top. Fill a plastic bag with some
water, knot the bag and add it on
top as a weight. Close the lid and
seal with the bracket. Place the jar
on a plate and ideally stand it in a
plastic bag since it is very likely that
some liquid will be ejected. Leave
the jar to stand at room temperature for 5–7 days.
// Put the jar in the refrigerator
for a few days. Remove from the
refrigerator, pour the contents into
a bowl and blend until smooth.
Strain the sauce through a coarse-
mesh strainer, then pour into
sterilised bottles. Keep in the
refrigerator.

Red cabbage sauerkraut

500 g (1 lb 2 oz) red cabbage
1½ teaspoons iodine-free salt
  (about 7 g)
1 apple (about 150 g/5 oz)
1 pinch of fennel seeds
1.5 litre (52 fl oz/6¼ cup) sterilised
  preserving jar with a rubber
  seal and bracket lock

// Shred the cabbage as finely
as possible, preferably with a
mandoline. Put the cabbage in
a bowl, sprinkle with salt and
knead thoroughly. Set to one side
for now.
// Rinse the apple and remove
the core (while retaining the skin).
Finely shred the apple, either using
a mandoline or a regular grater.
// Add the apple strips and fennel
seeds to the bowl containing the
cabbage and knead thoroughly
for about 10 minutes to ensure
that you remove liquid from the
cabbage.
// Add the cabbage mixture into
the glass jar a little at a time.
Apply pressure with a wooden
spoon to make everything fit. Finish
by pouring the cabbage liquid
from the bowl into the jar. Close
the lid and seal with the bracket.
// Place the jar on a plate and
ideally stand it in a plastic bag
since it is very likely that some
liquid will be ejected.
// Leave the jar to stand at room
temperature for 14 days. Then
leave it in the refrigerator for at
least 2 weeks to allow the flavours
time to properly develop.

Midsummer's Louisiana hot sauce

500 g (1 lb 2 oz) red jalapeños
1 tablespoon rapeseed (canola)
  oil
2½ teaspoons sea salt
2½ tablespoons water
100 ml (3½ fl oz/scant ½ cup)
  Champagne vinegar

// Cut the top off the jalapeños
and remove the core. Set aside
100 g. Put the remaining 400 g
in a bowl together with the oil. Stir
to ensure everything is covered.
// Light the barbecue and grill
the jalapeños on a high heat so
that they turn black on the outside
while the fire is still burning. Set
to one side and leave to cool
completely.
// Place all the chillies, salt and
water in a food processor or mixer
and blend until smooth. Pour
into a fermentation jar with a
water trap and leave at room
temperature for at least 6 weeks.
// Press the mixture through a
fine-mesh strainer. Add the vinegar
and fill sterilised glass bottles. The
sauce will keep in the refrigerator
for several years.

Tip: If you want a little more
of the smoky flavour, you can
buy burnt oak infusion spiral
(medium strength) that you
can add during step 3 of the
fermentation process. They are
available to buy from shops
that sell brewing and wine-
making equipment.

Classic light mushroom/ champignon broth

Makes 1.5–2 litres (52– 67 fl oz/6¼–8 cups)

600 g (1 lb 5 oz) mushrooms
1 medium onion
1 small carrot
1 leek, the dark green part
2 litres (67 fl oz/8 cups) cold
    water
3 garlic cloves
2 bay leaves
2 teaspoons white peppercorns
3 sprigs of parsley
2 sprigs of thyme
sea salt

// Finely chop the mushrooms, onion, carrot and the dark green part of the leek (it's also fine to use a food processor). Put the vegetables in a large saucepan, pour the cold water over them and bring to the boil. Crush the garlic and add to the saucepan along with the bay leaves and peppercorns. Lower the heat and leave to simmer for 45 minutes.
// Take off the heat. Add the parsley and thyme, stir a few times, cover with the lid and leave to stand for 20 minutes. Strain and season with a little salt.

Roasted mushroom broth

Makes 1½–2 litres (52 fl oz/ 6¼ cups)

600 g (1 lb 5 oz) mushrooms
4 garlic cloves
150 ml (5 fl oz/scant ⅔ cup)
    rapeseed (canola) oil
sea salt flakes and black pepper
1 yellow onion, coarsely chopped
1 small leek, coarsely chopped
1 carrot, coarsely chopped
200 ml (7 fl oz/scant 1 cup) white
    wine
2 bay leaves
2 litres (67 fl oz/8 cups) cold
    water
3 sprigs of parsley
2 sprigs of lovage

// Heat the oven to 225°C (440°F/gas 8). Cut the mushrooms into equal-sized pieces. Place the mushrooms and garlic cloves in a baking tray (pan) and drizzle over 100 ml of the oil. Season with salt and pepper. Roast in the middle of the oven for 20 minutes.
// Pour the rest of the oil into a large saucepan and put on a high heat. When it begins to smoke, add the onion, leek and carrot. Fry them on a high heat for 10–15 minutes so that they take on colour. Lower the heat a bit, add the wine and then the bay leaves. Add the mushrooms, then cover in water, bring to the boil and leave to simmer for around 1 hour.
// Remove the pan from the heat. Add the parsley and lovage and leave covered for another 20–30 minutes. Strain the stock into a mixing bowl and keep in the refrigerator or into an ice cube tray and freeze.

Vegetable broth

Makes 1½–2 litres (52– 67 fl oz/6¼–8 cups)

2 tablespoons rapeseed (canola)
    oil
1 yellow onion, coarsely chopped
1 small leek, coarsely chopped
1 carrot, coarsely chopped
1 celery stalk, coarsely chopped
½ fennel bulb, coarsely chopped
1 garlic bulb, halved and crushed
1 bay leaf
½ teaspoon white pepper
1 tablespoon white wine vinegar
2 litres (67 fl oz/8 cups) water
3 sprigs of parsley
2 sprigs of lovage

// Pour the oil into a large saucepan and put on a medium heat. Add all the ingredients except the vinegar, water, parsley and lovage and stir until everything is thoroughly mixed. Fry for 5–7 minutes until the vegetables soften. Stir occasionally so that the vegetables do not take on too much colour. Add the vinegar and stir. Raise the heat slightly, add the water and leave to cook for 1 hour.
// Remove the pan from the heat. Add the parsley and lovage and leave covered for another 20–30 minutes. Strain the stock into a mixing bowl and keep in the refrigerator or pour into an ice cube tray and freeze.

Shojin dashi using kombu, dried shiitake and roasted yellow peas

Makes about 2 litres (67¼ fl oz/8 cups)

60 g (2 oz) yellow peas
1 teaspoon rapeseed (canola) oil
½ teaspoon sea salt flakes
1.5 litres (52fl oz/6¼ cups) cold water
40 g (1½ oz) kombu (dead man's fingers also works well)
20 g (¾ oz) dried shiitake mushrooms

// Soak the peas overnight. Drain and transfer the peas to a saucepan. Add plenty of water and put the pan on a medium heat, bring to the boil and leave to cook for 1 hour. Drain, place the peas on a towel and allow them to steam off and dry. They should preferably be as dry as possible, so ideally pat down and dry the peas using another towel or paper towel.
// Heat the oven to 225°C (440°F/gas 9). Place the peas on a baking sheet, drizzle with oil and sprinkle with salt. Place in the oven for around 15 minutes until they are roasted and have taken on colour.
// Pour the cold water into a saucepan and add the seaweed and shiitake mushrooms. Put the pan in the refrigerator for around 5 hours.
// Remove the shiitake and set aside. Put the saucepan on a low heat and warm up the liquid to 65°C (150°F). Try to keep the temperature at this level as much as possible – it will rise and fall a little over time depending on your stove but try not to let it go much above 70°C (160°F). Add the shiitake to the pan and leave to stand at this temperature for 1 hour.
// Raise the heat and let the liquid reach a temperature of 90°C (195°F). Remove the shiitake and seaweed. Add the roasted peas and skim the foam that forms on the surface, turn off the heat and leave to stand for 30 minutes covered by the lid.
// Strain the liquid through a straining cloth.

Tips You can also make the dashi using something else roasted instead of yellow peas. Their function is largely to flavour the dashi and traditionally roasted soya beans are used.

Ramen noodles from SLURP

Serves 10

300 ml (10 fl oz/1¼ cups) water
1 tablespoon salt
10 g (½ oz) kansui or oven-roasted
  bicarbonate of soda (baking
  soda) (see tip below)
700 g (1 lb 9 oz/5¼ cups) plain
  (all-purpose) wheat flour
280 g (10 oz) ramen flour (can be
  replaced with wheat flour)
20 g (¾ oz) rye flour
potato flour or cornflour
  (cornstarch), for dusting

// Mix the water, salt and kansui
or bicarbonate of soda in a bowl
and stir until it has all dissolved.
// Put the flour into a food
processor and pulse several times
until the flours are mixed. Run the
food processor while slowly and
evenly adding the water. Stop
occasionally to scrape the mixture
from the sides if it gets stuck. The
dough is ready when it looks like
small, grainy bits. Cover with a lid
and leave to stand for 30 minutes.
// Knead the dough using an
electric pasta machine (it is very
heavy going if done by hand!).
Begin by running it through on
the roughest setting, then the
second, and finally the third. Fold
the dough and run it through the
biggest setting again. Repeat this
folding and rolling through the
largest setting two or three times,
or until the machine is working very
hard to process the dough.
// Cover the dough with cling film
(plastic wrap) when it is smooth
and silky, then leave to rest for
1 hour at room temperature. This
gives the gluten a chance to relax
and the dough 'matures', as
Japanese chefs like to put it.
// Flatten the dough and divide
it into pieces the right size to be
worked with the pasta machine.
Sprinkle a little potato or cornflour
over them and then run them
through the pasta machine until
they are the right thickness. Cut
them into strips as wide as you
like, and keep them in the
refrigerator until it is time to cook
them. They usually benefit from
resting for at least 24 hours.

**Tip: It can be tricky to find
kansui. You can use oven-
roasted bicarbonate of soda
(baking soda) as an alternative.
Heat the oven to 120°C (250°F/
gas ½). Spread the bicarbonate
of soda on a baking sheet
covered in baking parchment
and roast in the oven for
1 hour. Remove and allow to
cool before using the powder
and be careful when handling
the roasted variant as it can
irritate sensitive skin.**

Porcini mayonnaise

**Makes about 600 ml
(20 fl oz/2½ cups)**

100 ml (3½ fl oz/scant ½ cup)
   aquafaba
1 tablespoon porcini mushroom
   powder
1 tablespoon Dijon mustard
2 teaspoons vinegar, preferably
   Le Baume de Bouteville
1 teaspoon salt
1 pinch of black pepper
500 ml (17 fl oz/2 cups) rapeseed
   (canola) oil (not cold pressed)

Cashew mayonnaise

**Makes about 600 ml
(20 fl oz/2½ cups)**

100 ml (3½ fl oz/scant ½ cup)
   aquafaba
2 tablespoons cashew butter (see
   adjacent recipe)
2 teaspoons Champagne vinegar
1 teaspoon salt
1 pinch of white pepper
500 ml (17 fl oz/2 cups) rapeseed
   (canola) oil (not cold pressed)

Sriracha mayonnaise

**Makes about 600 ml
(20 fl oz/2½ cups)**

100 ml (3½ fl oz/scant ½ cup)
   aquafaba
2 tablespoons sriracha sauce
1 tablespoon Dijon mustard
1 teaspoon vinegar (12%)
1 teaspoon Japanese soy sauce
1 teaspoon sesame oil
500 ml (17 fl oz/2 cups) rapeseed
   (canola) oil (not cold pressed)

// Put all the ingredients for the mayonnaise except the rapeseed oil in a beaker or a tall, narrow bowl. Mix, using a hand-held blender, until everything is blended.
// Put the hand-held blender to the bottom of the bowl and add the rapeseed oil in a thin stream while mixing (hold the hand-held blender still at the bottom of the bowl). When you notice the mayonnaise starting to settle, pull the hand-held blender upwards Continue mixing to a good consistency.

Cashew butter and nut butters

// Several of the recipes in this book include various kinds of nut butter, include almond, cashew and hazelnut butters. These are available in all well-stocked supermarkets, but if you have a powerful food processor with a knife blade at home then it is very easy to make your own.
// Mix the nuts at top speed until you have an even and smooth butter. It takes 10–20 minutes, depending on your food processor, the type of nut and the quantity. At first, a nut flour is formed, but in due course the nuts release oil and you get a butter-like consistency. Make sure you have a spatula to hand so that you can scrape the nut pulp down from the edges. If it is still dry after 15–20 minutes of mixing, you can add a little extra oil – such as peanut (groundnut) oil, coconut oil or rapeseed oil – but don't use cold-pressed oil as the oil should be as natural in taste as possible.

Walnut milk

// Soak 155 g (5 oz/1¼ cups) of walnuts in 600 ml (20 fl oz/ 2½ cups) of water for 24 hours, replacing the water every 6 hours. Drain the liquid, trying to remove any shells that have come free from the nuts. Put the nuts in a food processor and add 300 ml water, then mix until as smooth as possible. Strain through a coarse-meshed sieve and pour into a glass jar or bottle. The drink can be stored for a few days in the refrigerator.

Pitch black Polish baguette

Serves 6

about 1 g fresh yeast
15 g (½ oz) activated charcoal
  powder
500 ml (17 fl oz/2 cups) cold
  water
750 g (1 lb 10 oz) strong plain
  (bread) flour, plus extra for
  dusting
¾–1 tablespoon coarse sea salt

// Dissolve the crumb of yeast and
the charcoal powder in water in a
large bowl (the contents will later
double in volume). Stir in 500 g
(1 lb 2 oz) of the flour and whisk
into a smooth batter. Cover with
a lid or cling film (plastic wrap)
and leave to rest for 12–16 hours
at room temperature. The temperature of the room will have
an impact on how quickly it
proves, so keep an eye on the
dough in the final hours. If you
notice that the bubbles are getting
smaller, this means it is losing its
edge. If so, move quickly onto the
next step.
// Add salt and the rest of the
flour into the dough. Knead the
dough using a stand mixer on a
medium speed for 8 minutes. Then
leave the dough to rest for 10 minutes, before working it for another
2 minutes. As you have got a head
start on the prove, there is really
no need for an intermediate
proving stage, but if you want to
you can leave the dough to rest
for 30 minutes – this will allow
the gluten in the flour to further
develop and the dough will
become more elastic and silky.

// Tip the dough onto a floured
surface. Cut it into 6 equal pieces
using a dough scraper (pulling
the dough apart with your hands
damages the gluten strands).
Shape the pieces of dough into
balls and leave them to rest for a
few minutes under a baking cloth.
// Gently shape the balls into
baguettes. If you notice the dough
beginning to crack, you can leave
them to rest a little longer to allow
them to recover. Flour the baking
cloth and put the first baguette
on it. Push the baking cloth gently
up against the baguette and lay
the next one beside it. Repeat this
process between each baguette to
ensure that they do not touch each
other but still benefit from support
to maintain their shape. Flour the
baguettes and cover with another
baking cloth. Leave to prove at
room temperature for 3–4 hours.
// Heat the oven to 250°C
(480°F/gas 9). Transfer the
baguettes onto a baking sheet
lined with baking parchment.
Place in the middle of the oven,
lower the heat to 230°C (450°F/
gas 8) and bake the baguettes
for around 20 minutes.
// Remove the baking sheet and
allow to cool. An important part
of the process is to let the steam
in the baguettes do its job, and if
you leave them for 30–40 minutes
this will produce the best crumb.

Danish pastries

Makes 10 pastries

400 g (14 oz/3 ¼ cups) strong
  plain (bread) flour with 11–12%
  protein, plus extra for dusting
70 g (2½ oz/⅓ cup) caster
  (superfine) sugar
2 teaspoons salt
175 ml (6 fl oz/¾ cup) cold water
90 g (3¼ oz) liquid sourdough
2 teaspoons fresh yeast
250 g (9 oz) vegan block or
  butter, for roll-out

// Day one: Mix all the ingredients except the butter by hand
by pinching them together with
your fingers in a mixing bowl until
everything comes together into a
dough. Tip it onto your counter
and knead for several minutes
to ensure that the dough is free
from any crumbs. Loosely wrap
the dough in cling film (plastic
wrap) and leave in the refrigerator
overnight.
// Day two: Remove the butter
from the refrigerator and leave
at room temperature for 30 minutes. Place it between two sheets
of baking parchment and pound
it with a rolling pin so that it becomes flat. Use a dough scraper
to cut the sides of the
butter so that it is an even square
with straight edges. Place any
butter offcuts on top of the square
and 'even' them out using the
scraper to make it an even square.
Place the slab of butter wrapped
in baking parchment into the
refrigerator for 15 minutes.

// Remove the dough from the refrigerator – it should have doubled in volume overnight. Flour your work surface and tip the dough onto it. Knock it down. Shape the dough into a rectangle of the same height as the butter but a little wider. Put the dough in the freezer for 15 minutes.

// Take out the dough and butter and place onto a lightly floured work surface. Roll out the dough so that it is twice as long as the slab of butter. Place the slab of butter in the middle of the dough and fold in the right and left sides of the dough towards the middle so that it envelops the butter. Pinch the dough at the joins so that no butter is visible. Flour the top of the dough and apply pressure to it with a rolling pin so that the butter and dough stick together. This will ensure that the butter stays with the dough when you roll it out.

// Turn the dough so that the line down the middle is horizontal. Roll the dough horizontally until it is four times as long. Do a four-fold by folding the outer edges towards the middle so that they meet. Then fold together the dough as if closing a book.

// Turn the dough 90 degrees and roll it out again to four times its length. Do another four-fold: fold the outer edges towards the middle so that they meet, and then once again fold together the dough as if closing a book. Wrap the dough in cling film and leave to rest in the refrigerator for 1 hour.

// Flour the dough and roll it out into a rectangle measuring 24 x 60 cm (10 x 24 in). Cut about 1 cm (¾ in) off the edges and then cut the dough into 10 squares measuring 11 x 11 cm (4¼ x 4¼ in). Then cut two 'L' shapes opposite each other, about 1 cm (¾ in) from the outer edges, so that the outer edge loosen but are joined together at the base. Then fold the right-hand corner down to the left and the upper to the lower.

// Place the Danish pastry on a baking sheet lined with baking parchment at least 5 cm (2 in) from the next pastry and leave to prove until twice the size. This should take about two hours in a switched off oven with some hot water at the bottom providing steam. Top any way you like and bake at 200°C (400°F/gas 6) for 20–30 minutes until they take on the colour you like.

Leve's pizza dough

Makes 6 pizzas

1 kg (2 lb 4 oz) strong plain (bread) flour
700 g (24 fl oz/scant 3 cups) + 75 ml (2½ fl oz/scant ⅓ cup) water at 40°C (105°F)
200 g (7 oz) active sourdough
20 g (¾ oz) sea salt

// Mix the flour, the larger quantity of water and sourdough by hand in a mixing bowl until the temperature of the dough is 30–33°C (86–91°F). Cover in cling film (plastic wrap) and leave to rest for 30 minutes. Add the salt and knead it into the dough together with remaining water. Leave the dough to prove at room temperature for 60 minutes. Fold the dough once every 20 minutes

while proving: moisten your hand and pick up the dough's outer edge, pull it carefully and fold it towards the middle. Continue until you have gone all the way around.

// Leave the dough in the refrigerator for 24 hours. During that time, the dough should increase in volume by 30–50% and feel airy, bubbly and lively. Place the dough on a floured baking board. Divide into pieces of around 300 g (10½ oz). Shape the pieces of dough into small balls but take care not to press too much air out of them. Sprinkle a little flour on each ball, cover them with a tea towel and then cover in cling film. Leave them to prove at room temperature for 1–2 hours.

// When the dough balls have finished proving, they should have slackened, sunk and increased around 20% in size. If you carefully push a finger into the dough and leave a small mark, the dough is ready to be made into pizzas.

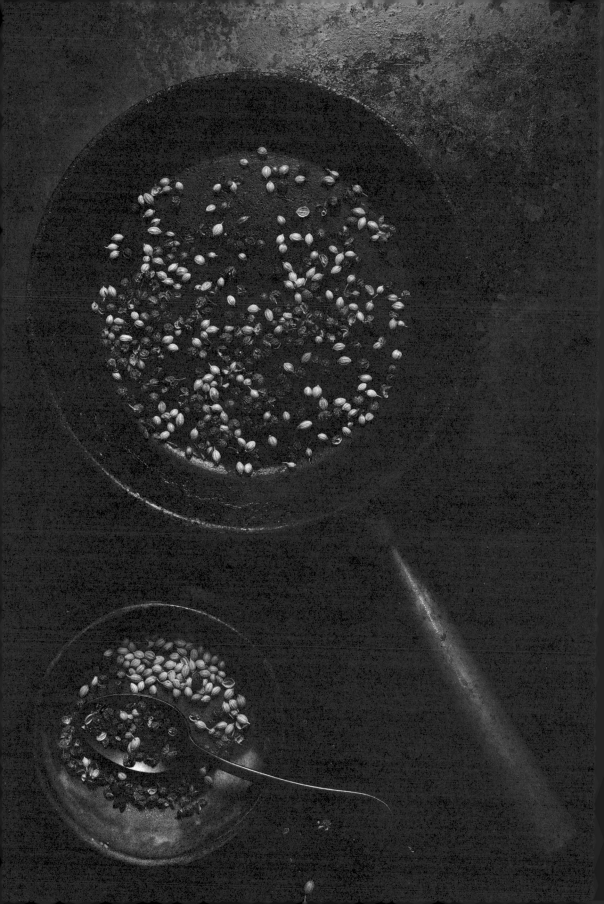

Mushroom and herb powders

// Making mushroom or herb powder is super-easy. Take any dried mushroom or herb you like and mix into a powder that is as fine as possible using a top-fed coffee grinder or a spice grinder. Put the powder in a sieve over a bowl and shake it so that you are left with the small, fine pieces of powder. Whatever is left in the sieve can be re-mixed so that everything eventually turns into a fine powder. Store in a dry, airtight container.

Black pepper spice

Makes 2 tablespoons

2 teaspoons coriander seeds
2 teaspoons Sichuan peppercorns
2 teaspoons whole black
   peppercorns

// Heat a cast-iron pan on a medium heat. Toast the spices until the seeds turn golden brown and you can clearly smell the spices.
// Crush everything into a fine powder using a mortar and pestle (a hand-held blender works well too). Store in a glass jar.

Whisky-pickled mustard seeds

Makes about 300 g (10½ oz)

4 tablespoons mustard seeds,
   preferably a mixture of yellow
   and brown
100 ml (3½ fl oz/scant ½ cup)
   apple cider whisky
110 g (3¾ oz/ ½ cup) cane sugar
   or caster (superfine) sugar
100 ml (3½ fl oz/scant ½ cup)
   water
3 tablespoons whisky
1 teaspoon salt

// Boil the mustard seeds in lightly salted water. Reduce the heat and simmer until the seeds are completely soft, which takes around 40–60 minutes. Strain the liquid.
// Boil the vinegar, sugar, water, whisky, salt and pre-boiled mustard seeds. Stir until the sugar has dissolved. Remove the saucepan from the heat and leave to cool.
// Transfer everything to a sterilised glass jar and keep in the refrigerator.

Roasted buckwheat

Makes about 200 g (7 oz)

160 g (5½ oz/scant 1 cup) whole
   buckwheat
1 tablespoon rapeseed (canola)
   oil

// Rinse the buckwheat in hot water and then cold water. Place in a mixing bowl, fill with water and leave to stand for at least 60 minutes.
// Strain and place the buckwheat on a tea towel and let it dry slightly.
// Put a frying pan (skillet) on a medium heat, add rapeseed oil and let it heat up. Add the buckwheat just before the oil begins to smoke. Fry the buckwheat for around 5 minutes until it turns crispy and golden brown. Stir occasionally to ensure it does not burn.

Handy storecupboard items

If you can't find some ingredients in the book on the shelves of your regular supermarket, pop into any well-stocked delicatessen or specialist to procure the following indispensable ingredients.

Soy sauce

I may use too much of it and too often, but it is such an incredible flavouring agent and it works beautifully with most mushrooms and in most dishes. Of course, there are many different variants from around Asia, and it can be fun to browse all the options and adjust your recipes based on what your personal preference is, but here is a selection of the ones I use most commonly.

Gen-en shoyu from Japan is a variant with half the usual salt content and goes well in marinades where you want lots of soy sauce. For some reason, I am very fond of the Korean soy sauce, ganjang, which is also great in broths and soups – just remember to use a bit less since it is slightly saltier. Tamari is another favourite with a very clear soy flavour, and if you mix it with miso the umami tones are incredible when you want soy with bells on. The same goes for shoyu, which also features a nice hint of roasted wheat in its flavour. For dumplings, I also use the Chinese sheng shou soy sauce, which also makes a great dipping sauce.

Vinegar

I really like to add vinegar to boost flavour towards the end of cooking a dish. Taste it and add what you think it needs to create a balanced dish. Sometimes, you may need to use more and sometimes you may need to use less than the recipe calls for depending on which vinegar you are using. Start with a few drops and then increase. A few of my favourites includes a great Chardonnay white wine vinegar, a malt vinegar for richer dishes, and when I'm quick pickling, Champagne vinegar is the shortcut to success. But it goes without saying that I also love experimenting with the Asian varieties that are usually based on rice rather than grapes. For dumplings and in a lot of my marinades, I like to use the dark shih chuan vinegar hailing from Taiwan, which has its own unique, delicious spicing characterised by sweet tones of orange and star anise. Another variety that stands out is hon-mirin, a sweet and mild Japanese rice vinegar. This can usually be replaced with rice vinegar, but it really is worth trying to find it!

Sesame oil

My favourite sesame oil is the roasted variety from Korea. But there are so many to choose from and some are milder and rounder in taste. Sesame oil can often be somewhat dominant in terms of flavour, so it is important to strike the right balance in each recipe so that it does not take over.

Peanut (groundnut) oil

This oil copes with really high temperatures and is a stand-out favourite when it comes to deep frying. The oil itself is quite tasteless, which means it does not compete with the flavours of the other ingredients.

Miso

I use miso as a flavouring agent in my kimchi base instead of fish sauce. Miso is available to buy in various forms from most Asian grocery stores, but you will also find it in some supermarkets. I generally use an organic, unpasteurised miso paste made from fermented corn and soybeans.

Sichuan pepper

Available in well-stocked grocers, this benefits from a floral, citrus-pepper flavour that verges on chilli. It is a great complement to coriander seeds and black pepper. There is also an oil made from toasted Sichuan peppercorns known as prickly oil, which can often be found in Asian grocery stores.

Seaweed

I am a convert to seaweed, which I use increasingly often as a way of adding flavour to broths – it is indispensable in the shojin dashi together with the dried shiitake. I also use seaweed frequently in soups, sauces, marinades and spices.

Dashi

Many recipes in this book contain shojin dashi as the base for the broth. It is a vegetarian version which according to custom uses dried shiitake mushrooms instead of bonito flakes (dried fish). However, if you do not have the time or energy to make the recipe shown on page 161, then there are ready-made vegetarian dashi powders available to buy in well-stocked grocery stores or online.

Chilli sauces

Fortunately, this is an area that has really blossomed in recent years, and you can now find delicious, hand-crafted chilli sauces everywhere – so do take the time to find one you like. Personally, I don't really like those that are too strong – chillies have an incredibly tasty, fruity taste that is lost when the sauce is too strong. A rather special type – characterised by its crispiness and oiliness – is Lao Gan Ma, which I love using in dumplings. I'm sure it can be made at home, but in this case I prefer to buy the original.

Espelette peppers

These are chilli fruits from the village of Espelette in the Basque country on the French side of the border. In my humble view, these are completely unparalleled when it comes to dried chilli spice. They give plenty of flavour and have just the right level of heat, unlike regular chilli powder, which is often typified by a somewhat harsh, overbearing chilli sting without much flavour. Espelette peppers are available from many delicatessens, but you can also buy them online.

Gochugaru

A Korean mild chilli and the classic red chilli used in kimchi. It also does very well in marinades and sauces together with soy sauce and sesame oil.

Nutritional yeast

I have started to use nutritional yeast more in mayonnaise, sauces, toppings and spices. It has a cheese-like, slightly nutty flavour and is a great vegan alternative to Parmesan.

Aquafaba

Aquafaba is the juice from cooking chickpeas (garbanzos) or straight from the can. I have tried many varieties of vegan mayonnaise, but aquafaba is still what I use most

often. Of course, liquid from other beans and so on will also work – use whatever you have to hand. And if you're making hummus don't forget to keep the liquid – it keeps for 4–5 days in the refrigerator and also freezes.

Shio koji

This is a liquid koji that is an umami catalyst in sauces and marinades. It also helps to make the texture of mushrooms and vegetables more tender if that is what you're after. Shio koji is usually available in Asian grocery stores but is also beginning to appear here and there in well-stocked delicatessens.

Whisky

Whisky and mushrooms ... surely the most delicious combination there is. I find that the well-rounded whiskies of Speyside with their soft honey sweetness often work best. Japanese malts can also have the same flavour profile. Of course, I've used the odd bourbon too, and that works fine. On the other hand, I keep away from the smoky whiskies of the Scottish west coast, which make for a harsh taste that is less pleasant – they are better suited to being drunk neat.

Activated charcoal powder

My recipe for dumplings on page 32 and the pitch black bread on page 168 feature activated charcoal powder. This is mainly for effect – the bread really does turn pitch black – but it also gives a pleasant flavour and is said to have cleansing properties, according to Japanese tradition. I order my charcoal online from a Danish company called Sort of Coal, who import activated charcoal from Japan that is made from charred pine bark.

Index

I doff my cap to all those of you who inspired, supported, encouraged and contributed to this book.

Thanks to Nicola, Anton and Ellie, my nearest and dearest, who have supported me through thick and thin (and, of course, served as guinea pigs for plenty of experiments) and made it possible for me yet again to safely bring another cookbook to fruition.

Thanks to my mother, Lena, for cooking such delicious mushrooms while I was growing up. I still find myself longing for those mushroom croustades, and it is quite possible that they are still the tastiest thing in existence. Thanks to my father, Björn, for being adventurous and taking us to so many restaurants while we were growing up, which left its mark and continues to form the basis of my culinary interests today. Thanks to my brother and sister for helping and supporting me, proofreading my work, checking photos and pushing me and giving me a boost when it was most needed.

Thanks to all my food pals! My old friends Christian and Alexander – you are more important than you realise. You are the reason why I do what I do, and you both still inspire me so incredibly much. Victoria, Viktor, Magnus and Matti, you are always there for me and up for various experiments and events, ready to chat about ideas and to help out, cooking the odd dish here and there. Pelle, thank you for your mentorship and all your support in my food journey. Rasmus, thank you too for your deliveries of wild garlic and for finally getting us up and running with filming our recipes!

Ola and Sebbe at Saltimporten, I'm so grateful that you share with me what inspires you and that you are always on hand to help. Alex at Midsummer Hot Sauces, thanks again for all our chats about fermentation and dashi and for sharing your chilli sauce recipe with me, (page 157). Thank you to bakers Martin and Didrik at LEVE bageri for all your support and skills, as well as the recipes for the doughs shown on pages 168–169. A hat tip to Karin – aka 'Chopstick Stories' – for lending me your crafting expertise and knowledge in the form of the most delicious dumplings there are (pages 32–37), as well as suggesting a new dream destination in the shape of Taiwan. Also Philipp and the gang at SLURP for providing the best noodles and ramen inspiration, as well as their recipe on page 164.

Thanks are also due to: Kala of Kala's kimchi for your inspiration and elevating my knowledge of Korean cookery to the next level. Sayan, for all our food chats but especially those about Thai cuisine, and for being so generous with all that is yours and providing the inspiration for the recipe on page 128.

In terms of all things mushrooms, special thanks to Mathias at Hällestad and Eva and the team at Solbacka for your expertise and for letting me immortalise your beautiful mushrooms and crops. Thanks to Bokeslundsgården, Vegostan and Los Perros urban farm for doing what you do so well and for all the verdant greens that come from your hands. Thanks to the Norrmans, Anna and Lars, for letting us stage a photoshoot in your beautiful green kitchen in the smithy. And thank you to all you talented potters and craftspeople who make beautiful things that elevate our food – not least Lotta at BadAss Ceramics and Emma at ljung by ljung.

Last but not least, Team Bonnier Fakta! Thanks to Eva for believing in me and taking a chance on me again for book three, as well as for your knowledge and dexterity. Thanks to Thomas for keeping everything in order and supporting me throughout the production process. Thanks to Li and Katy for their stunning design work. And thanks to Oskar for once again pitching in, taking portrait shots for the book and helping and supporting me in developing my craft as a food photographer.

Thank you!

First published in 2021 by Bonnier Fakta, Stockholm, Sweden
The English edition published in 2022 by Hardie Grant Books,
an imprint of Hardie Grant Publishing
Published in the English language by arrangement with Bonnier Rights,
Stockholm, Sweden

Hardie Grant Books (London)
5th & 6th Floors
52–54 Southwark Street
London SE1 1UN

Hardie Grant Books (Melbourne)
Building 1, 658 Church Street
Richmond, Victoria 3121

hardiegrantbooks.com

British Library Cataloguing-in-Publication Data. A catalogue record for this book
is available from the British Library.

Mushrooms
ISBN: 978-1-78488-553-3

10 9 8 7 6 5 4 3 2 1

For the Swedish edition:
Graphic design: Katy Kimbell and Li Söderberg

For the English edition:
Publishing Director: Kajal Mistry
Editor: Eila Purvis
Copy-editor: Wendy Hobson
Proofreader: Suzanne Juby
Translator: Ian Giles
Typesettor: David Meikle
Indexer: Cathy Heath
Production Controller: Sabeena Atchia

Colour reproduction by p2d
Printed and bound in China by Leo Paper Products Ltd.